AMERICAN EDUCATION

Its Men,

Ideas,

and

Institutions

Advisory Editor

Lawrence A. Cremin
Frederick A. P. Barnard Professor of Education
Teachers College, Columbia University

A MERICAN EDUCATION: *Its Men, Ideas, and Institutions*
presents selected works of thought and scholarship that have
long been out of print or otherwise unavailable. Inevitably, such
works will include particular ideas and doctrines that have been
outmoded or superseded by more recent research. Nevertheless,
all retain their place in the literature, having influenced educational thought and practice in their own time and having provided
the basis for subsequent scholarship.

THE EVENING SCHOOL IN COLONIAL AMERICA

By

ROBERT FRANCIS SEYBOLT

ARNO PRESS & THE NEW YORK TIMES
*New York * 1971*

Reprint Edition 1971 by Arno Press Inc.

Reprinted from a copy in
  The University of Illinois Library

American Education:
  Its Men, Ideas, and Institutions - Series II
ISBN for complete set: 0-405-03600-0
See last pages of this volume for titles

Manufactured in the United States of America

Library of Congress Cataloging in Publication Data

Seybolt, Robert Francis, 1888-1951.
    The evening school in colonial America.
    (Bureau of Educational Research. College of
Education. Bulletin no. 24) (American education:
its men, ideas, and institutions. Series II)
    Reprint of the 1925 ed.
    Includes bibliographical references.
    1. Evening and continuation schools--U. S.
--History. I. Title. II. Series: Illinois.
University. Bureau of Educational Research.
Bulletin no. 24. III. Series: American education:
its men, ideas, and institutions. Series II.
LC5551.S4 1971   374.8'73   78-165730
ISBN 0-405-03719-8

BULLETIN No. 24.

BUREAU OF EDUCATIONAL RESEARCH
COLLEGE OF EDUCATION

THE EVENING SCHOOL IN COLONIAL AMERICA

By

ROBERT FRANCIS SEYBOLT
Associate Professor of the History of Education
University of Illinois

PUBLISHED BY THE UNIVERSITY OF ILLINOIS, URBANA
1925

INTRODUCTORY STATEMENT

In issuing this account of the Evening Schools of Colonial America, the Bureau of Educational Research is serving merely in the capacity of publisher. The painstaking search for information relative to the practices in evening schools and the preparation of the report of the investigation is entirely the work of Professor Seybolt.

Through the publication of this bulletin important authentic information about the evening schools in colonial America is made available. As there was no systematic attempt to preserve facts relative to our early educational history, investigations of this type render a distinct service to historians of education and to others interested in the development of our present schools.

February 11, 1925.

WALTER S. MONROE, *Director,*
Bureau of Educational Research.

CONTENTS

PREFACE

This account of the evening schools in the American colonies is based on verifiable sources,—the newspapers. Nothing has been "read into" the records; they tell their story without urging. That some of the schools may have enjoyed an ephemeral existence does not detract from the value of the evidence. The large number announced in the advertisements of the period indicates the importance of the institution.

Only a few passing references will be made, in the first chapter, to the evening schools of New Netherland. They must be mentioned because they seem to have been the first in colonial America. The Dutch evening schools were not the progenitors of the evening schools in the English colonies; they were merely precursors.

CHAPTER I

EARLY ESTABLISHMENTS

The evening school in the American colonies is not a well-known institution. Its existence has remained hidden in sources not readily available for examination. The evening school occupied a prominent position in the educational life of the period, and, therefore, deserves more than passing mention. With the view of making its records more accessible to the student of early American education, this study will present a somewhat detailed, yet condensed, source-account of its essential features.

Available records indicate that the first evening schools in colonial America were those of New Netherland. Evening instruction enjoyed a well-established position in the institutional life of the Dutch colonists. The earliest reference to the practice is contained in the "Instructions and Rules for Schoolmaster Evert Pietersen, drawn up by the Burgomasters of this City" (New Amsterdam), dated November 4, 1661. In one section of these instructions, the following appears: "Besides his yearly salary he shall be allowed to demand and receive from every pupil quarterly as follows: For each child whom he teaches the a b c, spelling and reading, 30st; for teaching to read and write, 50st; for teaching to read, write and cipher, 60st; from those who come in the evening and between times pro rata a fair sum."[1] A record of November 17, 1668, reveals the fact that Wilhelmus La Montagne kept an evening school both "winter and summer," at Kingston.[2] Additional early references to evening schools, and provisions similar to those contained in the rules for Evert Pietersen, are to be found in the contracts of other Dutch schoolmasters subsequent to the first English occupation.[3]

---

[1]Minutes of the Orphan Masters of New Amsterdam (Translated by B. Fernow. 2v. New York, 1902, 1907), II, 115-116.

[2]Olde Ulster (Kingston, N. Y., 1905-   ), I, 237.

[3]Jacob Joosten, Flatbush, 1670, was "to receive in payment of A.B. and spelling, 2 gl; of reading and writing together, 2 gl., 10st; for evening school, reading and writing, 3 gl." (Flatbush Town Records, 105:207. Cited by Kilpatrick, W. H. The Dutch Schools of New Netherland and Colonial New York, 168.)

Dirk Storm kept an evening school at New Lotts, in 1681. (Flatbush Consistory Minutes, 49ff. Cited by W.H.K., 187.)

See Flatbush Consistory Minutes, 39ff. (cited by W.H.K., 172-173) for contract of Jan Tibout, whose service at Flatbush began on Dec. 18, 1681.

The contract of Johannes Van Ekelen, whose term of service at Flatbush began on Oct. 1, 1682, contains the following: "from those who attended the day school, for

Some of the Dutch schools continued, for a time, after New Netherland became the Royal Province of New York, in 1674, but were gradually replaced by those of the English.

The evening school appeared in the English colony of New York as early as 1690. A Harlem apprenticeship-indenture of that year contains the master's promise that his apprentice "shall have the privelege of going to the evening school."[4] An early reference to an evening school in New York City is found in an indenture of October 1, 1698, which bound the master to give the apprentice "his winter's schooling."[5] It will be shown later that "winter's schooling" referred, in most cases, to evening schools. A more definite record is an indenture of November 18, 1701, which contained the provision: "in the Evenings to go to School each Winter to the End he may be taught to write and read."[6] It is to be noted that the only sources of information concerning the evening school in New York, in the late seventeenth, and early eighteenth centuries, are indentures of apprenticeship. The writer found one hundred and eight New York City indentures, of the years 1698-1727, that refer to the practice of sending apprentices to evening schools. The distribution, in time, of this large number of separate references makes it safe to assume that the evening school was an accepted institution of the period mentioned. Some apprenticeship records indicate definitely that there was more than one evening school in New York City during this period. An indenture of October 17, 1705 contains the master's covenant "to lett him (the apprentice) have in Every Winter three Months Learning att any Evening School within this City, and to pay for the same."[7] Another master in 1720, agreed to send his apprentice "One Quarter of a year in each Year of the said Term to a good Evening School."[8]

---

a speller, or reader, three guilders a quarter, and for a writer, four guilders. From those who attended evening school, for a speller or reader, four guilders, and for a writer, six guilders shall be given." (Flatbush Consistory Minutes, 57-59. Cited by W.H.K., 174.)

See W.H.K., 190-191, for a brief treatment of the Dutch evening schools.

[4]Harlem Records, II, 529. (Manuscript folio, owned by the Title Guarantee and Trust Company of New York City.)

[5]Citty of N.Yorke Indentures, begun February 19, 1694 and ends Jan.ye 29th 1707, 47. (Manuscript folio, preserved at the city hall of New York City.) See also Harlem Records, II, 543; City of N.Yorke Indentures, 90, 81, 155; Liber 29, 19, 7, 31, 60, 67, 73, 117, 230, for indentures of 1698-1724. (Manuscript folio, labeled "Liber 29," containing "Indentures Oct. 2, 1718 to Aug. 7, 1727." Library of N. Y. Hist. Soc.)

[6]Citty of N. Yorke Indentures, 81.

[7]Ibid, 128.

[8]Liber 29, 80. (Dec. 29, 1720.)

Records at hand do not reveal the earliest date at which the evening school appeared in the city of Boston. For information concerning the early evening schools of New York, we may turn to the apprenticeship-indentures of the period. But such records are not available for a study of this type of instruction in Boston. In connection with a study of apprenticeship-education in colonial New England, the writer examined many Massachusetts indentures of apprenticeship, but did not find one in which provision was made for sending the apprentice to such a school.[9] It must not be inferred, however, from this lack of evidence, that evening schools did not appear in Boston as early as in New York City. It is highly probable that they were established in Boston before the close of the seventeenth century. Boston, like New York City, was a seaport, and a center of industry; and there must have been a similar demand for such schools. Furthermore, the schoolmasters of Boston were familiar with educational institutions in other colonies.

One of the earliest references to the evening school in Boston is contained in the following advertisement, in *The Boston Gazette*, for August 31-September 7, 1724:

This Evening Mr. Samuel Grainger begins his Evening School for Writing, Accompts, and the Mathematicks, such as intend to learn are desired to begin speedily and they shall be dispatcht with Expedition suitable to their Application.[10]

A notice in *The American Weekly Mercury* records the existence of an evening school in Philadelphia, in 1734.[11] The master of this school, Theophilus Grew, later became a "professor" at the Academy. Other early Philadelphia evening schools were established by Nathanael Platt, in 1742,[12] and, in the year following, by Joseph Crellius,[13] and Charles Fortesque.[14]

In Charleston, South Carolina, three evening schools were opened in 1744, by Jeremiah Theus,[15] Nathaniel and Mary Gittens,[16] and John Fouquet.[17] Fifteen years later, John Sims, "Schoolmaster in the

[9]Seybolt, R. F. Apprenticeship and Apprenticeship Education in Colonial New England and New York. Columbia University, New York, 1917.
[10]The Boston Gazette, Aug. 31-Sept. 7, 1724.
[11]The American Weekly Mercury, Philadelphia, Oct. 3-10, Oct. 31-Nov. 7, 1734. Repeated Oct. 16-23, 1735.
[12]The Pennsylvania Gazette, Mar. 31, Apr. 8, 1742.
[13]Ibid, Nov. 10, 16, 24, 1743.
[14]Ibid, Nov. 24, Dec. 1, 6, 15, 20, 1743.
Jacob Schuppy, 1743. (Ibid, Nov. 16, 24, Dec. 1, 15, 1743.)
[15]The South Carolina Gazette, Nov. 5, 1744.
[16]Ibid, Sept. 17, 1744.
[17]Ibid, Nov. 12, 19, 1744.

Town School" of Newport, Rhode Island, proposed "to open a separate School . . . beginning at half after Six O'Clock, and concluding at Eight."[18] In 1763, Maurice Towel, also of Newport, "resolved to begin just after the Holidays, and promises due Attendance either by Night or Day."[19]

The sources do not permit one to indicate definite dates for the establishment of the first evening schools in any of the colonies. It is evident that they were accepted institutions in the Dutch colony of New Netherland. In New York City, they appeared sometime between 1674 and 1700. Although documentary evidence has not come down to us, it may be supposed that such schools made their appearance in the important seaport cities of New England before the close of the seventeenth century. The earliest establishments in Philadelphia, and Charleston belong to the opening years of the next century.

---

[18]The Newport Mercury, May 22, June 5, 1759.
[19]Ibid, Dec. 26, 1763.

CHAPTER II

THE SCHOOL TERM, SEASONS, AND HOURS

Information concerning the school-seasons, and hours of attendance is abundant. Although the evidence is somewhat fragmentary in character, it is possible, by piecing together a large number of separate records, to build up a fairly complete account of this aspect of evening school practice.

One of the earliest references to an evening school in the English colonies occurs in a Harlem apprenticeship-indenture of November 25, 1690, in which the master promised that his apprentice "shall have the privelege of going to the evening school."[1] According to a New York City indenture of October 1, 1698, the apprentice was to be given "his winter's schooling."[2] From indentures of later date it is evident that the evening school in New York City, in the early eighteenth century, was kept in the winter. An indenture of November 18, 1701, contains the provision: "in the Evenings to go to School each Winter to the End he may be taught to write and read."[3] In some instances the master promised to give his apprentice "One Quarter of a Year's Schooling,"[4] in others "Every winter three Months Evening Schooling."[5] An indenture of January 20, 1720 combines the two preceding provisions by designating "a Quarter or three Months Schooling in every Winter."[6] And the particular three months, or quarter, during which the evening school was kept is indicated in an indenture of February 24, 1719, in which the master agreed "to put him to school three Months in Every Year during the said apprenticeship Immediately after Christmas . . . to the Evening

---

[1]Ch. I, n. 4.
[2]Ch. I, n. 5.
[3]Ch. I, n. 6.
[4]Citty of N. Yorke Indentures, 60. Indenture of Jan. 20, 1700.
See also indentures of 1718-1726, in Liber 29, 1, 39, 14, 54, 110, 123, 129, 152, 156, 181, 196, 199, 220, 227, 241, 244, 261, 264, 268, 270, 275, 284, 286, 303, 312, 314, 324, 325, 327, 354, 358.
[5]Citty of N. Yorke Indentures, 62, 107, 128, 143, 158.
See also indentures of 1701-1726, in Liber 29, 3, 13, 44, 45, 55, 59, 70, 86, 90, 102, 112, 119, 151, 158, 168, 172, 216, 232, 239, 242, 320, 349.
[6]Liber 29, 94.

School to learn to read and write."[7] Frequently the indentures refer to these three months as "the usual times in the Winter Evenings," or the "Customary" period.[8] An indenture of June 29, 1726 permits the apprentice "to go to School during the time that is customary here to keep Night School."[9]

Apprenticeship-indentures constitute our chief sources of information concerning the earliest evening schools in the colony of New York, those of the late seventeenth and early eighteenth centuries. But the evidence of these documents is somewhat incomplete, and it must be supplemented by reference to the newspapers, which began to make their appearance after 1725.[10] From that year on advertisements of evening schools are numerous, and they contain the only detailed accounts that have come down to us of any aspect of colonial evening school practice.

The indentures indicate that the earliest evening schools in New York City were kept only during the winter. This practice seems to have been continued by John Walton, of New York City, who announced, in 1723, that his "School from the first of October till the first of March will be tended in the Evening,"[11] and by James Lyde, whose advertisement of August 31-September 7, 1730 informs us that "On the 15th of September next" he "designs to Teach in the Evening (during the Winter)."[12]

[7]Liber, 29, 55. See also Citty of N.Yorke Indentures, 123, indenture of July 30, 1705: "to allow him Evening Schooling Every Winter from Christmas as is Customary;" Liber 29, 139, indenture of Jan. 18, 1721: "Schooling in Winter Evenings from Christmas;" Ibid, 289, indenture of June 1, 1725: "Every Quarter after Christmas;" Ibid, 346, indenture of May 1, 1726: "Eavening scholling from Christemis Eavery year of the said term."

[8]Liber 29, 34, 36, 102, 212, 216, 225. Indentures of 1717-1724.

[9]Ibid, 318.

[10]The New York Gazette, the first New York City newspaper, was established in 1725.

[11]The American Weekly Mercury, Philadelphia, Oct. 17-24, Oct. 24-31, Oct. 31-Nov. 7, 1723. There were no New York City newspapers at this date. Walton published his notice in a Philadelphia paper that circulated in New York.

[12]New York Gazette, Aug. 31-Sept. 7, 1730.

Gabriel Wayne: "will keep an Evening School during the Winter Season." (New York Gazette Revived in the Weekly Post Boy, Sept. 17, 24, 1750.)

Garrat Noel: "proposes to teach Night School during the Winter Season." (Ibid, Sept. 2, 9, 16, 23, 1751.)

Robert Leeth: "intends keeping an Evening School during the Winter." (Ibid, Sept. 18, 25, Oct. 2, 9, 16, 23, 30, 1752.)

John Lewis: "keeps a NIGHT SCHOOL, and purposes to continue it all the season." (N. Y. Gazette or Weekly Post Boy, Dec. 24, 1753; Jan. 7, 14, 21, 1754.)

Mr. Evans: "in the evenings during the winter." (Royal Gazette, Oct. 17, 20, 31, Nov. 21, 1781.)

J. Mennye: "EVENING SCHOOL...to be continued during the Winter." (New York Gazette and Weekly Mercury, Sept. 30, Oct. 14, 1782.)

[14]

Toward the middle of the century it was evident that school-masters, here and there in the city, were not observing the earlier custom of conducting evening schools only during the winter season. In a notice of May 4, 1747, "Thomas Metcalfe proposes to teach an Evening School . . . all the Summer."[13] A particularly pertinent advertisement, in this connection, is one inserted by Robert Leeth in the *New York Evening Post*, May 27, 1751:

I find it has been a Custom here immemorial, for School Masters to keep Evening Schools Winter only; But as it may suit many young People's Conveniencies to write and cast Accompts at other Seasons of the Year, I do hereby give Notice that I intend to keep an Evening School from six o'Clock till Eight, the Year round.[14]

There was no agreement among the masters that all the evening schools in the city should begin their terms at the same time. Thomas Evans announced, on December 18, 1749, that he had established himself "at the House of Mr. Bingham, Shoemaker, near the New-Dock, where he will give due Attendance for Night School, commencing the first Day of January next."[15] A New York City notice of September 15, 1755 announces that John Searson, "Who teaches School at the House of Mrs. Coon opposite to the Post Office, proposes (God Willing) to open an Evening School, on Thursday the 25th Instant September."[16] Thomas Johnson, on November 23, 1761, begged "Leave to inform the Public that he has this Day open'd a

[13]New York Evening Post, Aug. 3, 1747.
James Wragg: "Evening School continues all Summer." (N. Y. Gazette or Weekly Post Boy, Apr. 5, 12, 19, 26, May 3, 10, 17, June 14, 1756.)
James, and Samuel Giles: "during the Summer Season." (Parker's New York Gazette or Weekly Post Boy, Apr. 30, May 14, 21, 28, 1759.)
[14]N. Y. Evening Post, May 27, June 3, 1751.
[15]N. Y. Gazette Revived in the Weekly Post Boy, Dec. 18, 25, 1749; Jan. 1, 8, 1750.
Thomas Johnson: "this Day (Jan. 2) intends . . . to open an EVENING SCHOOL." (N. Y. Gazette, Jan. 18, 1762.)
James Gilliland: "will open a NIGHT SCHOOL, on Monday the 4th of January next." (N. Y. Gazette and Weekly Mercury, Dec. 14, 28, 1772.) Three years later, Gilliland announced "An EVENING SCHOOL To commence immediately after the Holidays." (Rivington's N. Y. Gazetteer, or Connecticut, Hudson's River, New Jersey, and Quebec Weekly Advertiser, Jan. 12, 19, 1775.)
[16]N. Y. Gazette or Weekly Post Boy, Sept. 15, 19, 29, Oct. 6, 13, 1755. Ibid, Oct. 27, 1755: "Night School is begun."
James Wragg: "Night School begins this Month." (N. Y. Gazette or Weekly Post Boy, Sept. 8, 15, 22, Oct. 6, 13, 1755.) Ibid, Oct. 20, 1755: "Night School is kept."
Edward Willett, and George Adams: "A Night School . . . will be opened on Monday September the Fourth." (N. Y. Gazette or Weekly Post Boy, Aug. 14, 28, Sept. 4, 1758.)
John Young: "purposes to open a Night School on the 21st Instant September." (N. Y. Mercury, Sept. 7, 1761.)
James Giles: "Evening School to begin September 20th." (N. Y. Gazette or Weekly Post Boy, Sept. 2, 23, 30, 1762.)
Samuel Giles: "will begin his Evening School on Monday the 24th instant." (Ibid, Sept. 20, 27, 1764.)

Day and Evening School,"[17] and Hugh Hughes, also of New York City, gave notice, on March 20, 1767, that he would "open a Morning and Evening School . . . to commence the first of April next, and to continue to the first of October following."[18]

A similar lack of uniformity obtained in New England with respect to the evening school seasons. *The Boston Gazette*, of August 31-September 7, 1724, contains a notice to the effect that "This Evening Mr. Samuel Grainger begins his Evening School for Writing, Accompts and the Mathematicks."[19] Charles Shimmin's evening school in Salem was announced on December 8, 1772, and on September 21 in the year following;[20] and in Marblehead, Peter Donworth gave notice on February 8, 1774 "that he has opened SCHOOL . . . His Hours for teaching are . . . from 5 till 8 of the Clock in the Evening."[21] Maurice Towel, of Newport, Rhode Island, in 1763, advertised to "begin just after the Holidays."[22] A Norwich,

[17]N. Y. Mercury, Nov. 23, 1761.

Edward Willett: "On Tuesday the First Day of November next a Day and Night SCHOOL will be open'd." (N. Y. Gazette or Weekly Post Boy, Oct. 24, 1757)

James Lamb: "night SCHOOL from the 1st of December." (Ibid, Dec. 12, 1768)

[18]N. Y. Gazette or Weekly Post Boy, Apr. 16, 23, 30, May 7, 14, 21, June 4, 1767.

[19]Boston Gazette, Sept. 4-11, 1727: "This Week Mr. Samuel Grainger begins Evening School." Ibid, Sept. 11-18, 1727: "Last Week Mr. Samuel Grainger began Evening School."

Boston Evening Post, Sept. 12, 19, 26, 1748: "Mr. Pelham's Writing and Arithmetick School...during the Winter Season."

John Vinal: "an EVENING SCHOOL will be opened the third Day of October." (Boston Gazette and Country Journal, Sept. 13, 27, 1756.) A year later, Vinal announced that "an Evening School will be opened the Second Day of October next." (Boston Post Boy and Weekly Advertiser, Oct. 9, 1758.) In 1759, his evening school opened on Oct. 1, "to continue till the 1st of April." (Green and Russell's Boston Post Boy & Advertiser, Sept. 10, 17, 24, 1759.) In 1776, Vinal appeared in Newburyport. Essex Journal and New Hampshire Packet, Oct. 25, Nov. 1, 1776: "John Vinal Intends to begin his EVENING SCHOOL for Youth of both Sexes the first Monday in November next."

John Griffith: "Intends to begin Evening School...the 19th Instant." (Boston Gazette and Country Journal, Oct. 5, 1767.)

[20]Essex Gazette (Salem, Mass.), Dec. 8-15, 15-22, 1772; Sept. 21-28, 1773.

Ibid, Oct. 25-Nov. 1, 1774: "Mr. Hopkins intends to open an Evening School Monday next, at 7 o'Clock."

Essex Journal and New Hampshire Packet, Oct. 25, Nov. 1, 1776: "Nicholas Pike Purposes to open his EVENING SCHOOL...on the first Monday in November next."

Ibid, Oct. 18, 25, Nov. 1, 1776: "Robert Long Determines to open an Evening School the first Monday in November next."

[21]Essex Gazette, Feb. 8-15, 15-22, 1774.

[22]Newport Mercury, Dec. 26, 1763.

John Sims: "proposes to open...on the first Wednesday of June next, to continue the Summer Season." (Ibid, May 22, June 5, 1759.)

Connecticut, "EVENING SCHOOL," of 1774, was also kept during the winter, by Thomas Eyre.[23]

The early evening schools of Charleston, South Carolina, seem to have been kept "during the winter season." A notice of 1744 "informs the Public" that Nathaniel and Mary Gittens "intend to commence an Evening School the 10th of September;"[24] and another, of the same year, that Jeremiah Theus' "Evening School . . . will be open'd on the first of November next."[25]

In Philadelphia, as in the other cities already mentioned, some of the evening schools were kept during the summer. It is worthy of remark that these schools were attended chiefly by girls, or "young Ladies." An advertisement of April 5, 1753 contains the announcement that an evening school for "young Ladies" would be opened, by William Dawson, "On Monday, the ninth of April."[26] Two years later, Dawson opened his "evening school for young Ladies" on "Monday, the 14th of April."[27] The same month was chosen by Joseph Garner for the opening of his school "for young Ladies only," in 1766.[28]

The most popular evening schools in Philadelphia were ·those that were conducted "during the Winter Season." It is a noteworthy fact that some agreement existed among the schoolmasters of that city with respect to the choice of the month in which to begin the winter term. A few schools were opened in September. N. Walton, and W. Hetherington announced, on August 15, 1745, that they would "open a Night School . . . the 10th of September next."[29] The school kept by "JAMES COSGROVE, with Assistants," in 1757, "was opened . . . on Monday the Fifth Instant" (September).[30] In most of the evening schools of colonial Philadelphia the "winter season" began in October, usually on the first, or second Monday.

[23]Norwich Packet and Connecticut, Massachusetts, New Hampshire, and Rhode Island Weekly Advertiser, Dec. 1, 8, 1774.
W. Harris: "Monday the 27th Instant." (Connecticut Gazette and the Universal Intelligencer, May 14, 1776.)
[24]South Carolina Gazette, Sept. 17, 1744.
[25]Ibid, Nov. 5, 1744.
[26]Pennsylvania Gazette, Apr. 5, 12, May 3, 31, June 14, 28, 1753.
[27]Ibid, Apr. 10, 1755.
[28]Ibid, Feb. 13, 1766.
[29]Ibid, Aug. 15, 22, 29, 1745.
[30]Ibid, Sept. 8, Dec. 8, 22, 1757.
Ibid, Sept. 18, 1766: "on Monday, the 29th Instant, will be opened an Evening Seminary."
Jacob Lawn: "French night school will be open again the 29th of this Instant." (Ibid, Sept. 24, 1783.)

October seems to have suggested itself as the proper month. The records refer to such opening dates as the first, fourth, fifth, sixth, eighth, thirteenth, and fifteenth of the month.[31] A relatively small number, in the eighteenth century, began their seasons after the fifteenth.[32] An excerpt from a printer's advertisement, of 1771, is especially pertinent in its reference to the uniformity that obtained with respect to the opening of the winter season. On October third, of that year, Henry Miller, "Printer, in Race-street, Philadelphia," announced that Blackmair's German Grammar "will soon be published . . . And, as *the Night Schools are to be opened this instant October*, both Masters and Scholars may have the Sheets at the aforesaid Editor's, as they come out of the Press weekly, in order to enable them to go through the Grammar against the Time of its Publication."[33] In 1772, the schoolmasters of the city met to discuss their evening school problems, and to determine a policy in this connection. The result of their deliberations is expressed in the following excerpt from the minutes, which were published, "By Order of the Meeting," in the *Pennsylvania Gazette*, September 30, 1772:

The Schoolmasters of this city and district, beg leave to inform the Public, that they intend opening NIGHT SCHOOLS, at their respective schoolhouses, on Monday Evening, the 5th of October next.

The length of the term appears to have been fairly definitely fixed by custom. From evidence of several kinds it may be inferred that most of the schools were run on a quarterly plan. There were a few, however, that were conducted on a different basis: John Walton's evening school, in New York City, in 1723, "from the first of October till the first of March will be tended in the Evening;"[34] Theophilus Grew, and Horace Jones, of Philadelphia, announced, in 1753, that they "intended an Evening School for this Winter Season . . . to commence on Monday, the 8th of October, and to continue until the Middle of March."[35] But these were exceptions; the five months term was not popular. Most of the indentures of apprentice-

---

[31]Oct. 1, 1754 (Dawson), 1771 (Fentham); Oct. 4, 1756 (Dawson, and Gladstone); Oct. 5, 1761 (Oliphant); Oct. 6, 1760 (Kennedy, Maxfield, and Kennedy), 1760 (Oliphant), 1766 (Thorne), 1766 (Power); Oct. 8, 1753 (Grew and Jones), 1753 (Dawson), 1770 (Oliphant), 1771 (Maguire, and Power); Oct. 13, 1766 (Thorne); Oct. 14, 1771 (Ellison); Oct. 15, 1770 (Stiles), 1770 (Ellison).
[32]David Ellison: "AN EVENING SCHOOL WILL be opened, on Monday, the 18th of October." (Ibid, Nov. 17, 1773).
A. Morton: "On Monday, the 24th of this Instant, October." (Ibid, Oct. 20, 1757.)
[33]Pennsylvania Gazette, Oct. 3, 1771.
[34]American Weekly Mercury, Oct. 17-24, 24-31, Oct. 31-Nov. 7, 1723
[35]Pennsylvania Gazette, Sept. 20, 27, 1753.

ship that refer to evening schools mention the "quarter" as the period, or term, of the schooling to be given the apprentices: "Every Winter one Quarter," "Every Quarter after Christmas." Some of the schools were kept "during the Winter Season," and others "during the Summer Season." It is evident, from an examination of the records, that these phrases referred either to a term of three months, or to one of six months, during the winter, or summer. The "customary" six months, or two-quarter, period is indicated in an advertisement published by John Vinal, of Boston, on September 13, 1756, in which he gave "Notice . . . That an EVENING SCHOOL will be opened on the Third Day of October . . . The said School to continue till the first Day of next April."[36] Additional evidence that evening schools were conducted on a quarterly basis is contained in advertisements that mention the rates of tuition; the various subjects were offered at so much "per Quarter."

An attempt to ascertain the evenings of the week on which these schools were kept reveals the fact that most of the records contain merely the apparently indefinite phrase "in the evenings." It may be assumed, however, that in such schools instruction was given every evening. A New York City advertisement, of 1772, announces that James Gilliland taught "every Evening."[37] Exceptions to this custom were indicated in but few instances. Joseph Garner, of Philadelphia, in 1766, kept "an Evening School . . . three Evenings in the Week."[38] He did not designate the evenings, in his announcement. Two New York City schoolmasters stated definitely that their schools would be open on certain evenings only: James, and Samuel Giles, in 1759, taught "in the evenings of all School Days, Wednesday and Saturday Evenings excepted;"[39] and John Nathan Hutchins, in 1763, omitted "Saturday evenings."[40]

The hours of instruction varied greatly throughout the colonies. In fact, there was no uniformity in this matter, in any one city. Thomas Metcalfe, of New York City, proposed, in 1747, "to teach an Evening School, beginning at five to be continued till Sunset."[41]

---

[36]Boston Gazette and Country Journal, Sept. 13, 27, 1756.
[37]N. Y. Gazette and Weekly Mercury, Dec. 14, 28, 1772.
[38]Pennsylvania Gazette, Feb. 13, 1766.
P. Webster: "on such Nights as shall best suit the Attendants." (Ibid, Dec. 18, 1766.)
[39]Parker's N. Y. Gazette or Weekly Post Boy, Apr. 30, May 14, 21, 28, 1759.
[40]N. Y. Mercury, Apr. 25, May 2, 1763.
Anthony Fiva: "Saturday excepted." (Rivington's N. Y. Gazetteer, or Conn., N. J., H. R., and Quebec Weekly Advertiser, May 19, 26, 1774.)
[41]N. Y. Evening Post, Aug. 3, 1747.

A Boston school, of 1748, was open "during the Winter Season. . . from Candle-light till Nine in the Evening as usual."[42] James Cosgrove, of Philadelphia, in 1755, "taught at the usual hours of evening schools."[43] In most cases the hours were definitely indicated as: "from 5 to 7 in the evenings," "from the hour of 5 to 8," "from 6 to 7 o'clock in the evenings during the Winter," "from 6 to 8 o'clock every Evening," and "from 6 to 9 in the Evening."[44] The most popular hours seem to have been from six to eight, and from six to nine.

Most of the evening schools in the American colonies were kept only "during the Winter." Although differences obtained in practice, the "usual" season was of six months duration, from October to April, and comprised two terms. These three-month periods were known as quarters, and constituted the term-basis of all colonial schooling. With but few exceptions, the schools gave instruction every evening in the week, classes beginning, in most instances, at six and ending at eight, or nine o'clock.

---

[42]Boston Evening Post, Sept. 12, 19, 26, 1748.

Ebenezer Dayton: "Night School ALL Summer, from Sun-set to 9 o'Clock." (Newport Mercury, Feb. 27-Mar. 6, 1769.)

[43]Pennsylvania Gazette, Feb. 4, 18, 1755.

[44]Five to seven: Platt (Phila.), 1742; J., and S. Giles (N. Y. C.), 1759; Hutchins (N. Y. C.), 1763. Five to eight: Donworth (Marblehead), 1774; Dawson (Phila.), 1753, 1755, 1756; Cather (Phila.), 1756. Six to seven: Evans (N. Y. C.), 1781. Six to eight: Webster (Phila.), 1766; Gilliland (N. Y. C.), 1772; Fiva (N. Y. C.), 1773; Gollen, and Mountain (N. Y. C.), 1774; Davis (N. Y. C.), 1778; Neil (Charleston, S. C.), 1783. Six to nine: Grew (Phila.), 1734, 1744; Pelham (Boston), 1748; Carroll (N. Y. C.), 1765; Dayton (Newport, R. I.), 1768; Shimmin (Salem), 1772; Daymon (Phila.), 1771; Fentham (Phila.), 1771; Nevell (Phila.), 1772.

John Sims: "beginning at half after Six O'Clock, and concluding at Eight." (Newport Mercury, May 22, June 5, 1759.)

CHAPTER III

THE CURRICULUM

According to the records, the curriculum of the earliest evening schools in the English colonies, those of New York City, consisted of reading, writing, and arithmetic. The evidence of the indentures of apprenticeship indicates that these subjects were studied separately, or in any combination desired by the apprentice, or his master. An indenture of October 14, 1700, provides for sending the apprentice to the "winter school to learn to read as long as the school time shall last."[1] In other instances the apprentice was permitted "in the evenings to go to School Each Winter to the End that he may be taught to write and Read,"[2] or to "Learn Writing and Cyphering at the usuall Winter Seasons."[3] The most popular provision, however, was: "One Quarter of a Year in Each Year of said Term to a good Evening School in Order to be well instructed in reading, writing, Accounting and the like."[4] The purpose of this education for apprentices is well expressed in the words of an indenture of December 7, 1724, which made provision for teaching the boy to "Read write and Cypher so far as will be Sufficient to manage his Trade."[5]

It may be of interest to note the content of the course in "cyphering," or arithmetic, pursued by the apprentice in this early period. A Westchester indenture, of July 1, 1716, makes provision for teaching the apprentice to "Read Write & Cast Accompts to so far as the

---

[1]Harlem Records, II, 543.

[2]Citty of N. Yorke Indentures, 81. Indenture of Nov. 18, 1701. See the following indentures in Liber 29: 59 (Feb. 9, 1719); 55 (Feb. 24, 1719); 69 (Dec. 9, 1719); 83 (Apr. 26, 1720); 119 (Nov. 18, 1720): "Every Winter...Evening School...to Read and Write;" 117 (Feb. 1, 1721): "Evening Schooling...to Read and write English;" 212 (July 10, 1722): "to read and write English...in Winter Evenings."

[3]Liber 29, 36. Indenture of Aug. 1, 1717. See the following in Liber 29: 36 (Aug. 1, 1717); 78 (Apr. 16, 1718): "Evening School...to learn to write and cypher;" 34 (Aug. 6, 1719); 102 (May 1, 1720): "School...Evenings to learn Writing and Cyphering;" 193 (Sept. 1, 1723): "Night School...writeing and Arithmetick."

[4]Liber 29, 80. Indenture of Aug. 1, 1720. See the following in Liber 29, 82 (Jan. 6, 1720): "Evening School...Reading and Writing and Arithmetick;" 190 (Nov. 6, 1722); 241 (Jan. 31, 1723): "Evening School to Read write and Cypher;" 197 (Aug. 1, 1723): "School...on Winter Evenings...to Read write and Cypher;" 266 (Dec. 25, 1723); 314 (Jan. 4, 1724); 225 (July 26, 1724); 278 (Oct. 5, 1724); 229 (Oct. 26, 1724); 280 (June 1, 1725); 289 (June 1, 1725): "to read and write...every Quarter...and Syfer two Quarters."

[5]Liber 29, 282.

Rule of three."[6] This usually meant the "Rule of Three Direct." Another statement of the composition of this subject occurs in a New York City indenture of May 20, 1720, in which the master agreed to provide instruction in "writing and cyphering so far as Addition Subtraction and Multiplication."[7] In some instances the apprentice was to be taught "to Cypher so as to keep his Own accounts,"[8] or "so far as he be able to keep his Books."[9]

Obviously, the evidence of the apprenticeship-indentures is somewhat incomplete. They indicate, in a matter-of-course manner, that evening schools were common in the Royal Province of New York during the late seventeenth, and early eighteenth centuries, and that the customary curriculum comprised reading, writing, and arithmetic. Additional light is thrown upon these schools by the newspapers; indeed, for this purpose, they constitute our best sources. After the establishment of the first colonial newspapers, advertisements of evening schools are numerous, and by piecing them together it is possible to build up a more complete account of the curriculum.

After the first quarter of the eighteenth century evening schools offering instruction only in the elementary subjects were comparatively few in number. Typical announcements of such schools are those of Peter de Prefontaine:

Philadelphia, October 30, 1746.
Reading, Writing, and Arithmetick, carefully taught, in the house where Jonathan Biles lately lived in Race-street, Philadelphia, almost opposite the Moravian Meeting-house: Where also is kept an evening school for the instruction of those who cannot come in the day-time, by me
Peter de Prefontaine.[10]

and of Thomas Evans, of New York City, December 18, 1749:

Reading Writing and Arithmetick, taught by Thomas Evans, at the House of Mr. Bingham, Shoemaker, near the New-Dock, where he will give due Attendance for Night School, commencing the first Dav of January next.[11]

Samuel Bruce, in 1761,[12] Thomas Wiley, from 1777 to 1782,[13] in New

[6]Westchester Records, 1707-1720, 254½. (Manuscript folio in New York Hall of Records.)
[7]Liber 29, 97.
[8]Ibid, 276. Indenture of Feb. 1, 1722.
[9]Westchester Records, 1711-1730. July 23, 1725. (Manuscript folio in New York Hall of Records. Pages not numbered.)
[10]Pennsylvania Gazette, Oct. 30, 1746.
[11]N. Y. Gazette Revived in the Weekly Post Boy, Dec. 18, 25, 1749; Jan. 1, 8, 1750.
[12]N. Y. Mercury, Aug. 31, Sept. 7, 28, 1761.
[13]N. Y. Gazette and Weekly Mercury, Feb. 17, 24, Mar. 3, 10, 24, 1777; Sept. 13, 20, 1779; Nov. 4, 1782.

York City; and William Payne, of Boston, in 1776,[14] taught only reading, writing, and arithmetic in their evening schools.

A few of the schools offered writing, and arithmetic only: for example, those of "Mr. Pelham," in 1748,[15] and John Griffith, from 1767 to 1771,[16] in Boston; Hugh Hughes, of New York City, in 1767;[17] and Lazarus Pine, of Philadelphia, from 1770 to 1773.[18] It may be surmised that these masters did not receive students who had not learned to read. This was undoubtedly true of Samuel Giles, of New York City, who appended the following to his advertisement of September 2, 1762:

N. B. It is evident from long Experience, that the teaching of small Children the first Rudiments is of ill Consequences in such a School (by taking up too much of the Teacher's Time). It is therefore proposed that for the Future, no Children will be taken but such as have already been taught to Read, and are fit for Writing.[19]

In other schools of this elementary type evening instruction was given in "writing, arithmetick, and to draw," by Nathaniel and Mary Gittens, of Charleston, South Carolina, in 1744,[20] and in "writing, arithmetic, and psalmody," by William Dawson, of Philadelphia, in 1756.[21]

It may be appropriate to remark, at this point, that the use of the term "elementary," to designate the rudimentary subjects, reading, writing, and arithmetic, is anachronistic. This technical acceptation of the word did not obtain, generally, in the colonial period; it belongs, rather, to a later day. The records refer to these subjects as the "lower branches," or the "rudiments."

Spelling, as a separate course of instruction, was rarely offered in the evening schools. Presumably, most of the students who attended these schools had already learned to spell.[22]

---

[14]New England Chronicle or Essex Gazette, May 2, 1776.
Ebenezer Dayton, Newport, R. I.: "Reading, Writing and Arithmetic." (Newport Mercury, Oct. 24-31, Oct. 31-Nov. 7, 1768.)
[15]Boston Evening Post, Sept. 12, 19, 26, 1748.
[16]Boston Gazette and Country Journal, Oct. 5, 1767; Oct. 3, 10, 17, 24, 1768; Oct. 14, 1771.
Massachusetts Gazette and Boston Weekly News-Letter, Oct. 1, 1772: "Writing and Arithmetic." (Master's name not given.)
[17]N. Y. Gazette or Weekly Post Boy, Apr. 16, 23, 30, May 7, 14, 21, June 4, 1767.
[18]Pennsylvania Gazette, Sept. 27, 1770; Sept. 26, 1771; Sept. 23, 1772; Sept. 22, 1773.
[19]N. Y. Gazette or Weekly Post Boy, Sept. 2, 23, 30, 1762.
[20]South Carolina, Gazette, Sept. 17, 1744.
[21]Pennsylvania Gazette, Apr. 15, 1756.
[22]William Milne, of Philadelphia, offered to give "half an hour each night at spelling without book, to such as pleases." (Pennsylvania Gazette, Oct. 17, 24, 1751.)
Robert Cather: "writing, arithmetick...the rules of spelling and reading with propriety." (Ibid, Mar. 25, 1756.)

In most evening schools of the colonial period writing, and arithmetic were taught with special reference to the trades, and commercial pursuits. The records indicate that these schools were established for apprentices, and others "who cannot attend in the day time." For many students of this type the course in writing would emphasize penmanship for clerical purposes. In 1745, N. Walton, and W. Hetherington, of Philadelphia, "taught Writing, in all the Hands of Great Britain."[23] Eight years later, William Dawson, also of Philadelphia, announced "A School to teach writing in all the hands of use," among other subjects.[24]

In the field of arithmetic, the distinction was made between "common, and mercantile arithmetic."[25] Common arithmetic obviously referred to the rudiments of the subject. The content of mercantile arithmetic is indicated, to some extent, by the advertisements of James, and Samuel Giles, of New York City, in 1759, who taught "Writing and Arithmetic both Vulgar and Decimal, Interest and Annuities, Extraction of Roots of all Powers;"[26] and Thomas Carroll, also of New York City, in 1765, who offered instruction in "Writing, Vulgar and Decimal Arithmetic; the Extraction of the Roots; Simple and Compound Interest; how to purchase or sell Annuities; Leases for Lives, or in Reversion, Freehold Estates, &c. at Simple and Compound Interest."[27] William Dawson, of Philadelphia, in 1753, taught "writing, arithmetic, vulgar and decimal, in a short and concise method, not commonly taught, whereby two-thirds of the time and trouble may be saved from the common methods; and such persons who have not time to go through the ordinary courses of arithmetic, may be made capable of common business by multiplication."[28]

[23]Pennsylvania Gazette, Aug. 15, 22, 29, 1745.
    Nathanael Platt, Phila., 1742: "will teach them all the most modish as well as necessary Hands." (Ibid, Mar. 31, Apr. 8, 1742.)
    Dunlap Adems, New York City, 1763: "Writing Master." (N. Y. Mercury, Jan. 10, 17, 24, May 9, 16, 1763.)
[24]Pennsylvania Gazette, Apr. 5, 12, May 3, 31, June 14, 28, 1753.
    Josiah Davenport, Phila: "Writing in all the different hands." (Ibid, Dec. 20, 27, 1753.)
    Alexander, and William Power, Phila: "WRITING, in all the modern hands." (Ibid, Sept. 30, 1772.)
    Benjamin Leigh, and Garrat Noel, New York City, 1751: "a new invented Short-Hand." (N. Y. Gazette Revived in the Weekly Post Boy, Jan. 21, 28, 1751.)
[25]John Heffernan, of Philadelphia, offered both "common and mercantile arithmetic." (Pennsylvania Gazette, Sept. 14, 1774.)
    George Fitzgerald, Phila: "mercantile arithmetic." (Ibid, Nov. 12, 19, 1783)
[26]Parker's N. Y. Gazette or Weekly Post Boy, Apr. 30, May 14, 21, 28, 1759.
[27]N. Y. Mercury, May 6, 13, 20, Sept. 30, Oct. 7, 1765.
[28]Pennsylvania Gazette, Oct. 4, 18, 1753.

The most popular evening schools of the eighteenth century offered instruction in practical subjects of higher grade, in addition to the rudiments. In these schools certain hours were "set apart" for those who were learning to read, write, and cipher. In schools of another type only the advanced subjects were taught. The higher classes were patronised not only by apprentices who had received an elementary education, but also by young men of means who were preparing for the vocations. Like the schools of purely elementary grade, they were designed for "those who cannot spare time in the day time."

The higher curriculum of these schools included a wide variety of courses. It will be found, on examining the evidence of the advertisements, that these schools met the demand of a large class for practical instruction beyond the rudiments. In schools of this type, open during the day, as well as in the evening, the book-keepers, merchants, surveyors, and navigators of the period received their technical training.

The typical higher, practical curriculum comprised book-keeping, or "Merchants Accompts," and "the practical Branches of the Mathematicks." Book-keeping occupied a prominent position among the vocational subjects of the colonial period. In a few instances, it is indicated, in the advertisements, merely by the word "accompts," or "accounts:" Samuel Grainger, of Boston, in 1724, offered instruction in "Writing, Accompts, and the Mathematicks,"[29] and Theophilus Grew, of Philadelphia, in 1734, taught "Merchants Accompts."[30] Additional light is thrown upon this subject by B. Leigh,

[29]Boston Gazette, Aug. 31-Sept. 7, 1724.
Nicholas Barrington, New York City, 1752: "Merchants Accounts." (N. Y. Gazette Revived in the Weekly Post Boy, Nov. 13, 1752.)
John Searson, New York City, 1755: "Merchants Accounts." (N. Y. Gazette or Weekly Post Boy, Sept. 15, 19, Oct. 6, 13, 1755.)
Edward Willett, New York City, 1757: "Merchants Accounts." (Ibid, Oct. 24, 1757.)
Thomas Johnson, New York City, 1761: "Merchants Accompts." (N. Y. Mercury, Nov. 23, 1761.)
John Young, New York City, 1761: "Merchants Accounts." (Ibid, Sept. 17, 1761.)
[30]American Weekly Mercury, Oct. 3-10, Oct. 31-Nov. 7, Dec. 5-12, 1734; Oct. 16-23, 1735; Sept. 20, 27, Oct. 11, 1744.
Grew, and Jones, Phila., 1753: "Writing, Arithmetick, Accompts." (Ibid, Sept. 20, 27, 1753.)
Charles Fortesque, Phila., 1743: "Merchants Accompts." (Ibid, Nov. 24, Dec. 1, 6, 15, 20, 1743.)
Joseph Stiles, Phila., 1754: "Merchants Accounts." (Ibid, Aug. 1, 22, 1754.)
William Thorne, Phila., 1766: "Merchants Accompts." (Ibid, Oct. 9, 16, 1766.)
Matthew Maguire, Phila., 1770: "READING, WRITING, ARITHMETIC, and ACCOMPTS." (Ibid, Oct. 25, 1770.)

and G. Noel, of New York City, who gave "Notice," in 1751, that they "taught Reading Writing, Arithmetick, and Accompts after the Italian Method of Double Entry;"[31] and by Edward Willett, and George Adams, also of New York City, who offered, in 1758, "Accompts, or the true Italian Method of Book-keeping."[32] Most announcements use some variation of the following: "Merchants Accompts according to the true Italian Method of Dr. and Cr. by Double Entry,"[33] or "Book-keeping after the true Italian Method."[34]

For an interpretation of "the practical Branches of the Mathematicks, an expression that appears frequently in the announcements, it will be necessary to examine a detailed advertisement, such as the following, of 1734:

> Over against the Post-Office in Second-street, Philadelphia, is taught Writing, Arithmetick in whole numbers and Fractions, Vulgar and Decimal, Merchants Accompts, Algebra, Geometry, Surveying, Gauging, Trigonometry, Plain and Spherical, Navigation in all kinds of Sailing, Astronomy, and all other Parts of the Mathematicks by THEOPHILUS GREW. His Hours are this Winter from 9 to 12 in the Morning; from 2 to 5 in the Afternoon; and (for the Conveniency of those who cannot come in the Day time) from 6 to 9 in the Evening. He teaches Writing, and Arithmetick at the usual Rate of 10s. per Quarter. Merchants Accompts, Navigation, &c. for 30s. per Quarter. And will undertake to furnish anyone with sufficient Knowledge in any of the foregoing Branches, in three Months time, provided the Person have a tolerable Genius and observes a constant Application.[35]

---

[31]N. Y. Gazette Revived in the Weekly Post Boy, Jan. 21, 28, 1751.
James, and Samuel Giles, New York City, 1759: "Book-keeping in the true Italian Manner of Double Entry." (Parker's N. Y. Gazette or Weekly Post Boy, Apr. 30, May 14, 21, 28, 1759.)
Samuel Giles, 1763: "Merchants Accompts in the Italian Method." (N. Y. Gazette or Weekly Post Boy, Apr. 21, 1763.) Samuel Giles, 1764: "Merchants Accounts in the Italian Method of Double Entry." (Ibid, Apr. 12, 1764.)
[32]N. Y. Gazette or Weekly Post Boy, Aug. 14, 28, Sept. 4, 1758.
[33]N. Walton, and W. Hetherington, Phila., 1745: "Merchants Accompts in the Italian Manner." (Pennsylvania Gazette, Aug. 15, 22, 29, 1745.)
Andrew Lamb, Phila., 1755: "Merchants Accompts in the true Italian Method of double Entry, Dr., and Cr." (Ibid, Oct. 23, Nov. 6, 1755.)
A. Morton, Phila., 1757: "Merchants Accompts according to the true Italian Method of Dr., and Cr. by double Entry." (Ibid, Oct. 20, 1757.)
Peter Donworth, Salem, Mass., 1774: "Book-keeping after the Italian Manner, or double entry." (Essex Gazette, Feb. 8-15, 15-22, 1774.)
[34]Robert Leeth, New York City, 1752: BOOK KEEPING after the true Italian Method." (N. Y. Gazette Revived in the Weekly Post Boy, Sept. 18, 25, Oct. 2, 9, 16, 23, 30, 1752.)
Thomas Carroll, New York City, 1765: "The Italian Method of Book-keeping." (N. Y. Mercury, May 6, 13, 20, Sept. 30, Oct. 7, 1765.)
Gollen, and Mountain, New York City, 1774: "book-keeping in the Italian method, by double entries." (Rivington's N. Y. Gazetteer, or Conn., N. J., H. R., and Quebec Weekly Advertiser, Oct. 6, 1774.)
J. Mennye, New York City, 1783: "Book-keeping according to the Italian Method." (Royal Gazette, Oct. 18, 22, 1783.)
[35]American Weekly Mercury, Oct. 3-10, Oct. 31-Nov. 7, Dec. 5-12, 1734.

A year later, Grew added to this notice "the use of Globes, Maps, Planispheres, Scales, Sliding-Rules, and all sorts of Mathematical Instruments."[36] As early as 1723, John Walton, of New York City, taught, among other subjects, "The Mariners Art, Plain and Mercators Way; also Geometry, Surveying."[37] A Boston notice of August 31-September 7, 1724 announced that "This Evening Mr. Samuel Grainger begins his Evening School for Writing, Accompts, and the Mathematicks."[38] In 1727, Grainger advertised an "Evening School, for Writing, Arithmetick, Book-keeping, Navigation, &c."[39] Additional information concerning this practical curriculum is supplied by the course of study offered by Charles Fortesque, of Philadelphia, in 1743, which included "Mensuration, Dialling, Geography . . . Chronology."[40] In a notice published by James, and Samuel Giles, of New York City, in 1759, mensuration appears as "mensuration of superficies and solids."[41] The curriculum announced by Edward Willett, and George Adams, of New York City, in 1758, contained, in addition to the subjects already mentioned, "Gunnery;"[42] and that of Robert Kennedy, John Maxfield, and David Kennedy, of Philadelphia, in 1760, "CONIC SECTIONS and STEREOMETRY."[43] "Fortification" is added by William Cock-

[36]American Weekly Mercury, Oct. 16-23, 1735.
    William Dawson, Phila., 1754: "the use of the Gunter's sliding-rule, necessary for most tradesmen, and others." (Pennsylvania Gazette, Sept. 19, Oct. 10, 1754.)
    Wm. Dawson, Phila., 1760: "all the necessary Branches of the Mathematics, with the Solution of every Problem by the plain or sliding Gunter." (Ibid, Nov. 20, Dec. 4, 1760.)
    Maguire, and Power, Phila., 1771: "the use of globes and maps; and how to make maps." (Pennsylvania Gazette, Sept. 12, 1771.)
    Alexander, and William Power, Phila., 1772: "the use of the globes, and maps." (Ibid, Sept. 30, 1772.)
[37]American Weekly Mercury, Oct. 17-24, 24-31, Oct. 31-Nov. 7, 1723.
    Andrew Lamb, Phila., 1755: "Great-Circle Sailing." (Pennsylvania Gazette, Oct. 23, Nov. 6, 1755.)
    Robert Leeth, New York City, 1755: "Great Circle Sailing." (N. Y. Gazette or Weekly Post Boy, May 12, 19, 26, 1755.)
[38]Boston Gazette, Aug. 31-Sept. 7, 1724.
[39]Ibid, Sept. 4-11, 11-18, 1727.
[40]Pennsylvania Gazette, Nov. 24, Dec. 1, 6, 15, 20, 1743.
    See also: Searson, N. Y. (N. Y. Gazette or Weekly Post Boy, Sept. 15, 19, 29, Oct. 6, 13, 1755): Wragg, N. Y. (Ibid, Apr. 7, 12, May 5, 1755): Hutchins, N. Y. (N. Y. Mercury, Apr. 25, May 2, 1763); Gilliland, N. Y. (N. Y. Gazette and Weekly Mercury, Dec. 14, 28, 1772); Mennye, N. Y. (Royal Gazette, Oct. 18, 22, 1783); Kennedy, Maxfield, and Kennedy, Phila. (Pennsylvania Gazette, Sept. 18, 25, Oct. 2, 1760)
[41]Parker's N. Y. Gazette or Weekly Post Boy, Apr. 30, May 14, 21, 28, 1759.
[42]N. Y. Gazette or Weekly Post Boy, Aug. 14, 28, Sept. 4, 1758.
[43]Pennsylvania Gazette, Sept. 18, 25, Oct. 2, 1760.
    William Ranstead, Phila., 1756: "Steriometry." (Ibid, Nov. 25, 1756.)

burn, of New York City, in 1764;[44] "Fluctions," by Alexander Power, of Philadelphia, in 1766,[45] and "the theory of pendulums" by John Wilson, of the same city, in 1772.[46] Wilson also taught "the construction of logarithms."

This comprehensive practical curriculum is admirably summed up in a Philadelphia notice of 1771:

An Evening School, for the following branches, kept by the subscriber in, Gray's-alley, near Dr. Thomas Bond's in Second-street, viz. Arithmetic, geometry, trigonometry, algebra, book-keeping, surveying, levelling, gauging, mensuration, dialling, geography, spherics, conics, navigation, astronomy, mechanics, hydraulics, hydrostatics, pneumatics, optics, perspective, architecture, fortification, gunnery, with the application and practical uses of each, in several trades and manufactures, in building all kinds of water-works, as docks, bridges, &c. also locks, sluices, and aqueducts for inland navigation; in the construction of various kinds of mills, and engines for abridging the labour of men; together with the most expeditious method of designing and drawing plans, elevations, sections, and perspective views in architecture, and to embellish the same, likewise exact methods of drawing any mill or engine, though of the most complex structure, so that another may be made similar thereto by any intelligent workman, with some other articles worthy of notice, too tedious to insert here.- - - A few sober, well disposed young men, who are desirious to apply diligently to any of the above branches, may be boarded upon reasonable terms by the subscriber, who will take particular care of the morals and behaviour of such as are intrusted to his care.

Christopher Colles.[47]

In the same year, Thomas Nevell, also of Philadelphia, gave evening instruction in "the art of architecture."

The practical purpose of geometry, and trigonometry is seen in their relation to navigation, and surveying. In the courses of study examined, they were usually allied with these two subjects. Several interesting records indicate this connection. In advertisements of 1753, and 1754, John Lewis, of New York City, announced that "What is called a new Method of Navigation, is an excellent Method of Trigonometry here particularly applied to Navigation; But is. of great Use in all kinds of Measuring and in solving many Arithmetical Questions."[48] James Cosgrove, of Philadelphia, in 1755, taught "geometry, trigonometry, and their application in surveying, navi-

---

[44]N. Y. Gazette or Weekly Post Boy, Jan. 12, Feb. 16, 1764.
[45]Pennsylvania Gazette, Oct. 2, 9, 1766.
[46]Ibid, Dec. 9, 1772.
John Heffernan, Phila., 1774; "logarithms." (Ibid, Sept. 14, 1774.)
J. Mennye, New York City, 1782-1783: "the Method of making Logarithms to any Number of Places will be taught, in as extensive a Manner as they have hitherto been in any University in Europe." (Royal Gazette, Oct. 18, 22, 1783.)
[47]Pennsylvania Gazette, Sept. 26, 1771.
See Appendix A for announcement by Thomas Carroll, New York City, 1765.
[48]N. Y. Gazette or Weekly Post Boy, Oct. 8, 15, Nov. 26, Dec. 3, 24, 1753; Jan. 7, 14, 21, 1754.

gation, &c,"⁴⁹ and Alexander Power, in 1766, "with their Appli-
cation to Surveying, Navigation, Geography, and Astronomy."⁵⁰
Another New York City master, William Cockburn, in 1764, offered
"Trigonometry, with its Application to the taking of Heights and
Distances . . . Spherical Trigonometry, with its Application to
Great Circle Sailing and Astronomy."⁵¹

In many of the advertisements, "the practical Branches of the
Mathematicks" are not enumerated as in the notices reproduced
above. Common abbreviations of this curriculum are "all Parts of
the Mathematicks," "any of the Branches of the Mathematicks,"
"all of the necessary Branches of the Mathematicks," and "the most
useful branches of the Mathematicks." James Lyde, of New York
City, in 1730, taught "in the Evening . . . Arithmetick, in all its
parts, Geometry, Trigonometry, Navigation, Surveying, Gauging,
Algebra, and sundry other of the said Parts of the Mathematicks;"⁵²
and Charles Shimmin, of Salem, Massachusetts, in 1772, "WRITING,
ARITHMETICK, NAVIGATION or any other Branch of the
MATHEMATICKS."⁵³ Other evening school advertisements use
the abbreviation "&c." in this connection: Samuel Grainger, and
John Vinal, of Boston, in 1727, and 1756, respectively, taught
"Writing, Arithmetick, Book-keeping, Navigation, &c.," and "Writ-
ing, Vulgar and Decimal Arithmetick, &c.&c."⁵⁴

The most popular of the "practical Branches of the Mathematicks" were surveying, and navigation. In fact, the demand for
instruction in these "branches" was so great, that they were early
elevated to the status of independent subjects.

Throughout the colonies there were many evening schools other
than those belonging strictly to the types just considered. One interesting institution was the evening "academy," a good illustration
of which is given in the following announcement, of October 17-24,
1723:

There is a School in New York, in the Broad Street, near the Exchange, where
Mr. John Walton, late of Yale Colledge, Teacheth Reading, Writing, Arethmatick,
whole Numbers and Fractions, Vulgar and Decimal, The Mariners Art, Plain and Mercators Way; Also Geometry, Surveying, the Latin Tongue, the Greek and Hebrew
Grammers, Ethicks, Rhetorick, Logick, Natural Philosophy and Metaphysicks, all or

---

⁴⁹Pennsylvania Gazette, Feb. 4, 18, 1755.
⁵⁰Ibid, Oct. 2, 9, 1766.
⁵¹N. Y. Gazette or Weekly Post Boy, Jan. 12, Feb. 16, 1764.
⁵²N. Y. Gazette, Aug. 31-Sept. 7, 1730.
⁵³Essex Gazette, Dec. 8-15, 15-22, 1772; Sept. 21-28, 1773.
⁵⁴Boston Gazette, Sept. 4-11, 11-18, 1727.
Boston Gazette and Country Journal, Sept. 13, 27, 1756.

any of them for a Reasonable Price. The School from the first of October till the first of March will be tended in the Evening. If any Gentlemen in the Country are disposed to send their Sons to the said School, if they apply themselves to the Master he will immediately procure suitable Entertainment for them, very Cheap. Also if any Young Gentlemen of the City will please to come in the Evening and make some Tryal of the Liberal Arts, they may have opportunity of Learning the same Things which are commonly Taught in Colledges.[55] This is the earliest available record of an "academy" in the American colonies.

An appreciable number of evening schools offered instruction in the ancient languages. John Walton, cited in the preceding paragraph, advertised "the Latin Tongue, the Greek and Hebrew Grammers." In 1743, Charles Fortesque, of Philadelphia, gave instruction in "The Latin Tongue," in addition to the practical subjects.[56] Latin, and Greek appear in the evening courses announced by Thomas Metcalfe, of New York City, in 1747;[57] Robert Kennedy, John Maxfield, and David Kennedy, of Philadelphia, in 1760;[58] and Peter Donworth, of Marblehead, Massachusetts, in 1774.[59] "JOHN HEFFERNAN, TEACHER of the MATHEMATICS and the ENGLISH Language," in Philadelphia, 1774, taught "Latin grammar, and a few of its subsequent classics, with a concise but comprehensive method of parsing."[60]

Evening schools offering instruction in the modern languages were by no means uncommon. A Philadelphia advertisement of November 10, 1743, announces that Joseph Crellius "designs to open his Winter Evening School on Monday the 21st Instant, where the German Language will be taught in a plain and easy manner to such Gentlemen as desire to be instructed therein."[61] In the same

---

[55]American Weekly Mercury, Oct. 17-24, 24-31, Oct. 31-Nov. 7, 1723. This "academy" antedated the Philadelphia Academy by twenty-eight years.
[56]Pennsylvania Gazette, Nov. 24, Dec. 1, 6, 15, 20, 1743.
See also: James Cosgrove, Phila. (Ibid, Feb. 4, 18, 1755.); Francis Daymon, Phila. (Ibid, Apr. 25, Oct. 3, 1771; Apr. 14, 1773.)
[57]New York Evening Post, Aug. 3, 1747.
See also: B. Leigh, and G. Noel, New York City (N. Y. Gazette Revived in the Weekly Post Boy, Jan. 21, 28, 1751); John Lewis Mayor, New York City (N. Y. Gazette or Weekly Post Boy, Oct. 8, 15, Nov. 26, Dec. 3, 1753; Sept. 30, Oct. 14, Nov. 4, 11, 1754); Timothy Wetmore, New York City, (N. Y. Gazette and Weekly Mercury, Jan. 27, 1777).
[58]Pennsylvania Gazette, Sept. 18, Oct. 2, 1760.
[59]Essex Gazette, Feb. 8-15, 15-22, 1772.
[60]Pennsylvania Gazette, Sept. 14, 1774.
See also: Gabriel Wayne, New York City, (N. Y. Gazette Revived in the Weekly Post Boy, July 30, Aug. 6, 13, 27, 1750); Robert Leeth, New York City (Ibid, Sept. 18, 25, Oct. 2, 9, 16, 23, 30, 1752); Thomas Ross, New York, City (N. Y. Mercury, Oct. 7, 1754).
[61]Pennsylvania Gazette, Nov. 10, 16, 24, 1743.

year, John Schuppy, also of Philadelphia, called attention to the fact
that "the German and French Languages are greatly improved on in
Europe," and, he added "it's not question'd but will be so here."[62]
Schuppy conducted a "German Evening School" in Philadelphia
during the years 1743-1745. Another well-known teacher of German
in Philadelphia was Jacob Ehrenzeller, who "opened" an "Evening
School" in 1756.[63] In a notice of 1766, Ehrenzeller "takes this Method,
humbly to return Thanks to the Gentlemen whom he had the Honour
to instruct in the German Language these many years."[64] In addition
to French, and Latin, Thomas Ross, of New York City, in 1754,
taught "LOW-DUTCH."[65] Obviously, the demand for German in
Philadelphia, and Low Dutch in New York City was influenced by
local conditions.

There seems to have been a steady demand for evening instruction in French, Italian, Portuguese, and Spanish. Benjamin Leigh,
and Garrat Noel, of New York City, in 1751, offered "the French,
Portuguese, and Spanish Languages,"[66] and Anthony Fiva, from 1773
to 1775, "French, Spanish, and Italian."[67] French, by far the most
popular foreign language in the American colonies, was taught by
many masters who also gave instruction in other subjects.[68] A well-
established institution for "Young Gentlemen and Misses, and
Adults of both Sexes" was the "French Night School." In 1744,
John Fouquet, of Charleston, South Carolina, opened a "French

[62]Pennsylvania Gazette, Nov. 16, 24, Dec. 1, 15, 1743; Sept. 20, 27, 1744; Sept.
26, 1745.
    Seybolt, R. F. "Some Notes on the Teaching of German in Colonial Phila-
delphia," in The Journal of English and Germanic Philology, Vol. XXIII, No. 3,
p. 418-421.
    [63]Ibid, Sept. 30, 1756.
    [64]Ibid, Oct. 30, 1766.
    Jacob Ehrenzeller, Phila., 1770: "continues to teach the GERMAN LANGUAGE
and promises to exert, to the utmost of his Power, all his Skill and Diligence, in the
Execution of his Duty, to the Satisfaction of his Scholars." (Ibid, Dec. 13, 1770.)
    Jacob Lawn, Phila., 1783. (Ibid, Sept. 24, 1783.)
    [65]N. Y. Mercury, Oct. 7, 1754.
    [66]N. Y. Gazette Revived in the Weekly Post Boy, Jan. 21, 28, 1751.
    [67]Rivington's N. Y. Gazetteer, or Conn., N. J., H. R., and Quebec Weekly Adver-
tiser, July 22, Aug. 12, Dec. 9, 16, 1773; May 19, 26, Dec. 22, 1774.
    [68]John Lewis Mayor, New York City, 1753-1754: "French, Latin and Greek."
(N. Y. Gazette or Weekly Post Boy, Nov. 26, Dec. 3, 1753; Sept. 30, Oct. 14, Nov. 4,
11, 1754.)
    Thomas Ross, New York City, 1754: "FRENCH, LOW-DUTCH, LATIN."
(N. Y. Mercury, Oct. 7, 1754.)
    Gollen, and Mountain, New York City, 1774: "the French and other languages,
&c. &c." (Rivington's N. Y. Gazetteer, or Conn., N. J., H. R., and Quebec Weekly
Advertiser, Oct. 6, 1774.)
    Francis Vandale, New York City, 1775: "French and other languages." (Ibid,
Oct. 26, Nov. 9, 16, 1775.)

Evening School for young Gentlemen at 40s. per Month."[69] A New York City advertisement, of 1757, gave notice that "Young Gentlemen and Ladies may be taught the FRENCH language in a Manner the most modern and expeditious by one lately arrived from London, who has made his Tour through France."[70] Other French evening schools, in New York City, were kept by John Girault, in 1771-1772,[71] John Haumaid, in 1772-1773,[72] M. Teniere, in 1777,[73] and Thomas Egan, in 1780;[74] and in Philadelphia, by William W. Fentham, in 1770,[75] and Jacob Lawn, in 1783.[76] French was considered a "very fashionable and necessary language" in the eighteenth century.

Before the middle of the eighteenth century the curricula of the evening schools included such subjects as algebra, astronomy, book-keeping, chronology, dialling, English, ethics, French, geography geometry, German, Greek, gauging, Hebrew, history, Latin, logarithms, logic, metaphysics, natural philosophy, navigation, rhetoric, surveying, and trigonometry.

There was no evening school curriculum as such. Each school had its own offering of subjects, and this was determined either by local demand, or by the qualifications of the masters. Obviously, no student took, in any one "season," all of the courses offered in the more comprehensive curricula announced by some of the masters. The subjects were elected singly, or in any combination desired by the students.

It is evident that some of the schools were distinctly elementary in character. But few were what could be termed "secondary." Most of the evening schools offering instruction in the higher subjects included the rudiments as well.

---

[69] South Carolina Gazette, Nov. 12, 19, 1744.
[70] N. Y. Gazette or Weekly Post Boy, Oct. 17, 24, 1757.
[71] N. Y. Gazette and Weekly Mercury, Sept. 9, 16, 23, 1771.
John Philipse, New York City, 1758. (N. Y. Gazette or Weekly Post Boy, Jan. 30, Feb. 6, 20, Mar. 6, 1758.)
[72] N. Y. Gazette and Weekly Mercury, Sept. 21, 1772.
[73] Ibid, Sept. 1, 8, 15, Oct. 6, 13, 20, 1777.
[74] Ibid, Jan. 10, 1780.
[75] Pennsylvania Gazette, Nov. 29, Dec. 27, 1770.
Francis Daymon, Phila., 1770-1773. (Ibid, Nov. 29, Dec. 20, 1770; Feb. 21, Apr. 25, Sept. 5, Oct. 3, 1771; Apr. 14, June 9, Nov. 17, 1773.)
[76] Ibid, Sept. 24, 1783.

CHAPTER IV

METHODS OF INSTRUCTION

References to the methods of instruction employed in the evening schools are not very numerous, and the few that are to be found in the records are rather indifferent in character. However, it may be profitable to examine some of the statements made by the masters themselves.

But little information is to be gained from announcements to the effect that certain subjects will be taught "carefully," "with the greatest care and diligence," "in a plain, practical, and concise Method," and "according to the most modern and improved Methods." John Young, of New York City, in 1761, taught "Reading, Writing, Arithmetick, and Merchants Accounts in the newest and most concise Methods hitherto taught in this City,"[1] and Charles Shimmin, of Salem, Massachusetts, in 1772, "WRITING, ARITHMETIC, NAVIGATION . . . according to the best and most approved Methods now taught in England."[2] Nothing more definite is contained in most of the records.

The masters stated, in some instances, that their methods would be adapted to the abilities of their students. In Samuel Grainger's evening school, in Boston, 1724, "such as intend to learn . . . shall be dispatcht with Expedition suitable to their Application."[3] John Sims, of Newport, Rhode Island, announced, in 1759, that "he endeavours to study the Genius of his Scholars, whether of exalted or inferior Capacities, and conducts himself accordingly."[4] They do not reveal any of the details of their class-room technique, however.

Only a few of the notices throw more light upon the matter, and these offer but a glimpse of the methods used in teaching such subjects as Latin, German, French, English, surveying, navigation, and book-keeping.

The records indicate that instruction in Latin was adapted to the practical, as well as the purely cultural requirements of the

---

[1] N. Y. Mercury, Sept. 7, 1761.
[2] Essex Gazette, Dec. 8-15, 15-22, 1772; Sept. 21-28, 1773.
[3] Boston Gazette, Aug. 21-Sept. 7, 1724.
[4] Newport Mercury, May 22, June 5, 1759.

students.[5] Frances Daymon, of Philadelphia, appears to have taught the language with reference to the needs of druggists, and physicians. In a notice of November 29, 1770, he announced that "The Youth who have no leisure to spend a long time in learning Latin; as Surgeons, Apothecaries, Druggists, Chymists, &c. may be taught in that branch of learning with the greatest expedition, after the manner of the two learned and celebrated gentlemen Mr. Locke, and Mons. Crousaz, that is, with little grammar, in which the too diffusive and intricate rules are wholly useless for that purpose."[6]

German was taught "according to the Rules of the Syntax" by Jacob Ehrenzeller, Philadelphia's best known teacher of "this necessary and useful Language."[7]

Anthony Fiva, of New York City, who advertised, in 1773, that he "continues to teach grammatically . . . the French, Spanish, and Italian Languages," announced to his prospective pupils that he would "ground them both in the true accent of these polite languages, and all the rules of the syntax."[8] His notice of 1774 contains the additional information that he taught these languages with the view of fitting "his pupils in a short time to carry on an epistolary correspondence, so useful particularly to young persons in business."[9] French was offered by John Philipse, of New York City, in 1758, "according to Mr. Paillaret's System;"[10] and John Girault, who kept a "French Night School," in New York City, in 1773, instructed "his pupils in all the variations of this polite tongue, after the rules of the most approved grammars, founded on the decisions of the Academy at Paris."[11] A Philadelphia "Master of the French, Latin, &c.," who also taught "in the newest and most expeditious Method,

[5]Charles Fortesque, Phila., 1743: "likewise intends for the future to instruct his Latin Scholars in Writing himself." (Pennsylvania Gazette, Nov. 24, Dec. 1, 6, 15, 20, 1743.)

James Cosgrove, Phila., 1755: "Latin by the newest and most effectual methods." (Ibid, Feb. 4, 18, 1755.)

John Heffernan, Phila., 1774: "Latin Grammar, and a few of its subsequent Classics, with a concise and comprehensive method of parsing." (Ibid, Sept. 14, 1774.)

[6]Pennsylvania Gazette, Nov. 29, 1770.

[7]Ibid, Oct. 30, 1766.

[8]Rivington's N. Y. Gazetteer, or Conn., N. J., H. R., and Quebec Weekly Advertiser, Dec. 9, 1773.

In 1774, Fiva "Informs his friends...That he still continues teaching the above languages...after the manner of academies, universities, and colleges of the learned world." (Ibid, Dec. 22, 1774.)

[9]Ibid, May 19, 26, 1774.

[10]N. Y. Gazette or Weekly Post Boy, Feb. 6, 20, Mar. 6, 1758.

[11]Rivington's N. Y. Gazetteer, or Conn., N. J., H. R., and Quebec Weekly Advertiser, Sept. 16, 23, Oct. 7, 14, 1773.

agreeable to the latest Improvements of the French Academy," announced, in 1771, that he "proposes to bestow a Gold Medal in the beginning of May next, to that Scholar, who shall, in the presence of competent judges, translate English into French with the greatest facility, and who shall be best acquainted with the idioms and genius of that language."[12]

English was usually taught "grammatically;" in fact, grammar as a foundation for all advanced work in "English reading and speaking" received a great deal of attention during the eighteenth century. As early as 1743, English was taught, in an evening school, "in a grammatical Manner," by Charles Fortesque, of Philadelphia.[13] A long advertisement by Hugh Hughes, of New York City, in 1772, throws considerable light upon the methods of teaching the subject:

To the PUBLIC

THE SUBSCRIBER proposes, if encouraged, to teach the English Language grammatically. And, for the Satisfaction of those who may be disposed to encourage such a necessary Mode of Education as that of instructing Youth in the grammatical Knowledge of their native Tongue, confessedly is, he gives the following Sketch of a Plan which he has adopted. When the Pupil can read fluently and write a legible Hand, he will be taught the English Accidence, or the Properties of the Parts of Speech, as divided and explained in the latest and most eminent English Grammarians; that is DOCTOR LOWTH, DOCTOR PRIESTLY, and others. After which he will be taught how to parse disjunctively, then modally, and instructed in the Rules of English Syntax; and, when he is sufficiently skilled in them to account for the Construction of the Sentences in general, he will receive Lessons of false Spelling and irregular Concord, &c. taken from some classic Author, but rendered ungrammatical for the Purpose of trying his Judgment. When he has reduced these as near their Originals, as his Knowledge of Grammar will permit, he will be shown all such irregularities as may have escaped his Notice, either in the orthographical or syntactical Part. These Lessons will also be selected from different Authors on various Subjects; and frequently from the Works of those who are the most celebrated for the Elegance of their Epistolary Writings; as this Kind of Compositon is acknowledged to be as difficult as any, and of greater Utility. The erroneous Part in every Lesson will likewise be modified. At one Time, it will consist of false Spelling alone. At another of only false Concord. The next perhaps, will consist of both. The 4th may not be composed of either of them, but may contain some Inaccuracies, or Vulgarisms &c. The 5th may retain all the foregoing Improprieties, and the last, none of them, of which the Pupil needs not be apprised, for Reasons that are too evident to require a Recital. To the preceding Exercises will succeed others on the Nature and Use of Transposition - - The Ellipses of all the Parts of Speech, as used by the best Writers, together with the Use of synonymous Terms - - A general Knowledge of all which joined to Practice, will enable Youth to avoid the many orthographical Errors, Barbarisms, inelegant Repetitions, and manifest Solecisms, which they are otherwise liable to run into, and in

[12]Pennsylvania Gazette, Oct. 3, 1771.
[13]Ibid, Nov. 24, Dec. 1, 6, 15, 20, 1743.
  Alexander Power, Phila., 1766 (Ibid, Oct. 2, 9, 1766); Joseph Garner, Phila., 1766 (Ibid, Feb. 13, 1766); John Beard, Phila., 1783 (Ibid, Oct. 8, 15, 22, 1783); Joseph Ward, Boston, 1772 (Mass. Gazette and Boston Weekly News Letter, Oct. 1, 15, 1772); Peter Donworth, Marblehead, 1774 (Essex Gazette, Feb. 8-15, 15-22, 1774).

Time, render them Masters of an easy elegant Style by which means they will become capable of conveying their Sentiments with Clearness and Precision, in a concise and agreeable manner; as well with Reputation to themselves, as Delight to their Freinds - - Lastly tho' the Pointing of a Discourse requires riper Judgment, and a more intimate Acquaintance with the syntactical Order of Words and Sentences than the Generality of Youth can be possessed of, to which may be added, the unsettled State that Punctuation itself is really in; so that very few precise Rules can be given, without numerous Exceptions, which would rather embarrass than assist the Learner; Yet, some general Directions may be given, in such a Manner as greatly to facilitate so desirable an Acquisition; and they will be attended to on the Part of the Tutor, in Proportion to the Susception of the Pupil. But he doth not mean to insinuate that the most tractable of mere Youth can be perfected in all the Varieties of the Language in a few Quarters, as Perfection is not to be acquired by Instruction alone, any more than it is by Practice without Instruction. On the Contrary he knows that it is a Work which requires considerable Time and much Labour, on the Part of the Teacher; and that all hasty Performances in Grammar, have a greater Tendency to raise a slender Superstructure than lay a permanent Foundation. Much more might be said on the Advantage resulting from this Mode of Education, were they not so very plain, that they scarcely require mentioning, and that this is only a Sketch. However, it may not be amiss to observe, that the Pupils by continually searching of their Dictionaries in Quest of Primitives and their Derivatives, as well as the constituent Parts of compound Terms; besides learning the Dependence that native Language has on itself; will also treasure up in their Memories a vast Stock of Words from the purest Writers; And, what is of infinitely more Value, their just Definitions, as every One of this Class will have Johnson's Dictionary in Octavo. Therefore, if it be true, that 'He who knows most Words, will have most Ideas,' and that on the 'Right Apprehension of Words depends the Rectitude of our Sentiments,' May it not be presumed, that such a Plan, in its full Extent, bids fair for improving the Minds of Youth in Necessary Knowledge, and consequently, is likely to produce intelligent Men and useful Citizens? The Consideration of which, is, with all due Deference most humbly submitted to the respectable Public; by its greatly obliged and very humble Servant,

H. Hughes.

P. S. He intends, as soon as Opportunity will permit, to publish a series of Ratios; calculated for converting by Multiplication alone, any Sum of New-York Currency, or the Currency of any other Colony, into Sterling; but may be equally useful for finding the Value of a lower Currency in a higher; when the difference between them increases, or decreases, as it does between Sterling and Currency.

N. B. His Night School will be opened on Monday Evening the 6th of Jan., 1772.[14]

John Heffernan, an evening school master of Philadelphia, in 1774, taught "grammatic English, with due attention to emphasis, pause, cadence, and puerile declamation."[15] John Davis, of New York City, in 1778, exercised "the greatest care, not only that they shall learn to read grammatically, but be taught properly and syntactically; whence they can discover the beauty and elegance of their mother tongue; that they may be able to construe what they read,

---

[14]N. Y. Gazette and Weekly Mercury, Dec. 30, 1771; Jan. 6, 13, 20, 27, 1772.
George Fitzgerald, Phila., 1783: "The English language, according to Louth and Sheridan's grammar rules." (Pennsylvania Gazette, Nov. 12, 19, 1783.)
Gollen, and Mountain, New York City, 1774 (Rivington's N. Y. Gazetteer, or Conn., N. J., H. R., and Quebec Weekly Advertiser, Oct. 6, 1774).
[15]Pennsylvania Gazette, Sept. 14, 1774.

thro' every part of speech. By this means, the scholar is fully taught to understand the science of what he reads; and, is able to express himself with propriety."[16] Another notice, of a New York City evening school, may be of interest, at this point, in which the following is included:

The English Language, agreeably to the Rules laid down by the most approved Grammarians, and that the Memory may be as little burthened as possible, the Rules are compressed in as few Words as the Nature of the Subject will permit; and, in order that no Inconveniency may arise from this Conciseness, a greater Variety and Number of Examples are given to the Scholars, by way of Exercises than are to be met with in any English Grammar yet published; Besides, that no Illustration of the Rules which can possibly be wanting, many Passages will be produced from our most celebrated Authors, to prove, that they themselves, have in many Instances, proved themselves to have been ignorant or inadvertant to several of the Rules which are now universally received as Canons; whence this Inference may fairly be drawn, that English Grammar has hitherto been too much neglected.[17]

According to most of the notices, surveying was taught "both in Theory and Practice." A brief additional note is supplied by Thomas Carroll, of New York City, who announced, in 1765, that he would teach "Surveying in Theory, and all its different Modes in Practice, with two universal Methods to determine the Areas of right lined Figures."[18]

The teaching of navigation receives a more satisfactory treatment in the records. References to this popular subject are both numerous, and detailed. John Walton, of New York City, in 1723, gave instruction in "The Mariners Art, both Plain and Mercators Way."[19] A notice published by Andrew Lamb, of Philadelphia, in 1755, emphasizes the practical character of the course, by calling attention to the importance of keeping a "Journal." It follows:

WRITING, Arithmetick, Vulgar and Decimal Fractions, &c. Merchants Accompts the true Italian Method by double Entry, Dr. and Cr. Navigation in all its Parts, both Theory and Practice, &c.- - - Also Spherical Trigonometry, Great-Circle Sailing, Astronomy, Surveying, Guaging, &c. and a compleat Method to keep the Ship's Way at Sea, called a Journal, whereby I teach in my School, to find the Longitude at Sea every Day at Noon, by true Proportions; as sure as the Latitude by Observation of the Sun; I have the originals to Produce, in which it will appear the Plan is like a Chain, the first Link of which being fixed to the Port departed from; each Day's Work a new Link joined to the other, till the last Link is fixed to the Port arrived at; each Day's Work being truly wrought, the Journal is compleat. My Journals from England to Cape Henlopen (or Cape James) in America; and from thence to the

---

[16]N. Y. Gazette and Weekly Mercury, Jan. 19, 26, 1778.
[17]Royal Gazette, Oct. 18, 22, 1783.
[18]N. Y. Mercury, May 6, 13, 20, Sept. 30, Oct. 7, 1765.
G. McCain, Phila., 1766: "The Theory and Practice of Surveying and Navigation, both according to the best Authors now in Print." (Pennsylvania Gazette, Aug. 7, 1766.)
[19]American Weekly Mercury, Oct. 17-24, 24-31, Oct. 31-Nov. 7, 1723.

Lizard Point again, I have proved to be within one Degree of Longitude, (near 140 Degrees of West Longitude) as appears in my Journals to be produced, with others of the like Sort, and are good Proofs of my Principles; although Sun and Stars should disappear for several Days and Nights, my Plan will find both Latitude and Longitude at Noon every Day, or any other Hour; it is a rational Plan and founded upon great and long experience at Sea, both on board the Royal Navy and Merchant Ships. Sailors take Care you be not abused by Land men pretending to this Plan.

N. B. I have taught Navigation, and kept a Journal above 40 Years; the Scheme is new and never was in printed Books, and has been approved by proper Judges, &c. Your log-line must be 50 Feet between each Knot, and Glass just 30 Seconds; or your Log-line may be 48 Feet between each Knot, and Glass just 29 Seconds. I give due Attendance at my School in Front-street at John Johnston's, Tallow Chandler, next Door to Mr. Richardson, Goldsmith, up the Alley. And teach both Day and Night-School, or wait upon any Gentleman at his Chamber, &c.

ANDREW LAMB.[20]

His namesake, James Lamb, of New York City, in 1768, could also give his students the benefit of actual experience at sea; "he has had 16 Years Experience at Sea," and "flatters himself he can render Navigation (in some Measure) familiar to the young Navigator the first Voyage."[21] An important method in Andrew Lamb's "Plan," that of finding "both Latitude and Longitude at Noon every Day, or any other Hour," was also emphasized by William Cockburn, of New York City, 1764, who offered "a new Method of observing the Latitude at any Time of Day, so very much wanted in thick Weather at Noon."[22]

David Ellison, of Philadelphia, in 1771, taught "Navigation in all branches, both with regard to theory and practice, with the construction and use of a true Sea Chart (according to the oblate spheroid figure of the earth) whereby the errors attending the other projections are avoided, and how to find the latitude at sea, by two altitudes of the sun, at any time of the day, and to find the longitude at sea, by the altitudes and distances of the sun and moon, or a known fixed star and the moon."[23] This method of finding the latitude and longitude was "exhibited in John Hamilton Moore's Navigation," according to an announcement by "Mr. Evans," of New York City, in 1781.[24] In 1773, Ellison offered "the solution of the problem for finding the longitude at sea by celestial observation; also to find the latitude by the moon's meridional altitude."[25]

[20]Pennsylvania Gazette, Oct. 23, Nov. 6, 1755.
[21]N. Y. Gazette or Weekly Post Boy, Dec. 12, 1768.
[22]Ibid, Jan. 12, Feb. 16, 1764.
[23]Pennsylvania Gazette, Oct. 17, 24, 1771.
[24]Royal Gazette, Oct. 17, 20, 31, Nov. 21, 1781.
[25]Pennsylvania Gazette, Nov. 17, 1773.
Davis, New York City, 1782: "Practical Navigation by the most expeditious and approved methods, whereby the Navigator can never be at a loss upon any occasion,

Robert Leeth, of New York City, in 1755, taught "the Construction of the Plain and Mercator's Chart on the same Sheet, which cannot but give the young Artist a clearer Idea of the Error of the One and the Truth of the other,"[26] and Thomas Carroll, in 1765, "the Construction and Use of the Charts, and Instruments necessary for keeping a Sea-Journal with a Method to keep the same, were the Navigator deprived of his Instruments and Books &c. by any Accident."[27]

In most of the evening schools of the colonial period, merchants accounts, or book-keeping, was taught "after the Italian Method of Double Entry." Alexander, and William Power, of Philadelphia, in 1772, offered "BOOK-KEEPING in the newest and most approved method now taught in Dublin,"[28] and George Fitzgerald, in 1783, "according to Dowling's system, which is allowed to be the most accurate method now extant in Europe." Fitzgerald advised "gentlemen who intended their children for mercantile business" that "his method of instruction" was "adapted to real trade."[29]

For purposes of illustration, actual journals, or ledgers, were examined, and analyzed in the evening classes of John Heffernan, of Philadelphia. He taught, in 1774, "Italian book-keeping, with sundry domestic, foreign, and company accompts demonstratively journalized."[30]

An occasional exception to, or criticism of, the Italian method is to be found in the advertisements. William Dawson, of Phila-

---

to find the ship's place, by dead reckoning and celestial observation, and to this purpose also are taught the doctrine of the Orthographic and Stereographic Projection of the Sphere, Spheric Trigonometry, with its application to Astronomy, by which he will be led to the summit of his wishes, it being supposed, a thorough knowledge of the New Method of finding the Latitude by two altitudes of the Sun, and of finding the Longitude by the Moon's distance from the Sun, &c." (N. Y. Gazette and Weekly Mercury, Jan. 7, 14, Oct. 14, 21, 1782.)

J. Mennye, New York City, 1783: "Navigation, together with the new Method of finding the Latitude and Longitude will be taught in a short Time to those who are already acquainted with Figures. Likewise the Method of making a Chart, fitted to any Voyage." (Royal Gazette, Oct. 18, 22, 1783.)

[26]N. Y. Gazette or Weekly Post Boy, May 12, 19, 26, 1755.

[27]N. Y. Mercury, May 6, 13, 20, Sept. 30, Oct. 7, 1765.

[28]Pennsylvania Gazette, Sept. 30, 1772.

[29]Ibid, Nov. 12, 19, 1783.

"At the new Academy...an Evening Seminary," Phila., 1766: "Merchants Accounts so effectually as to render the Pupil qualified to enter a Compting House." (Ibid, Sept. 18, 1766.)

Davis, New York City, 1782: "Book-keeping in the exemplary manner, so that the Book-keeper can adapt his ideas to any circumstances in trade and business." (N. Y. Gazette and Weekly Mercury, Jan. 7, 14, Oct. 14, 21, 1782.)

[30]Pennsylvania Gazette, Sept. 14, 1774.

delphia, in 1755, for example, taught book-keeping "by way of single entry, in a plain and methodical manner."[31] In the same year, John Searson, of New York City, announced that "as 'tis evident it would be too tedious and require too much Leisure and time for the Shopkeeper and Retailer to keep to all the Rules of Merchants Accompts," he "proposes to teach a very short and perspicuous Method for Retails &c. to adjust their Accompts by."[32] An interesting criticism was published by George Robinson, of New York City, in 1770:

This is to inform the Public, That
George Robinson,

Late of Old England, purposes opening an EVENING SCHOOL, at his house on Golden Hill, New York, January the 8th for book-keeping as used in London, either in the wholesale or retail way: Has practised it upwards of twenty years, having served an apprenticeship in the mercantile way, and ever after constantly used to it. Presumes it necessary almost every Person intended for business should learn a course of book-keeping; but begs leave to say, not in the customary way: Witness the complaints among merchants and tradesmen, that their boys when they first come to business, are almost as ignorant in the management of their books as if they had never learnt any method. There is boys who have not had time to learn, or perhaps a capacity to understand a compleat course of the Italian, which is commonly promiscuously alone taught to all; there are also many intended fo# such business as that the Italian method is thrown away upon them. Hours from 6 to 8.[33]

In some of the schools the younger students were separated from the older ones. Alexander, and William Power, of Philadelphia, in 1772, had "two large rooms on the same floor, one of which will be for the reception of young men, and others who would not choose to study in a crowded school, composed of boys of every denomination. Pupils of more tender years, in the adjoining room, will have a double advantage by being separated, because they can be properly classed, the school not so much hurried, and they not liable to be imposed on by those of riper years."[34]

Another feature of class-room technique is indicated by the practice of limiting the number of students. Thomas Carroll, of New York City, in 1766, would not "crowd his School with more than he can teach at a Time."[35] In this connection, Matthew Maguire, of Philadelphia, made the following announcement, in 1770: "I am determined to take no more than such a number as I shall be able to give proper attendance to."[36]

An "Evening Seminary" announcement of Philadelphia, in 1766, contains the information that "Examinations will be held every

[31]Pennsylvania Gazette, Apr. 10, 1755.
[32]N. Y. Gazette or Weekly Post Boy, Sept. 15, 19, 29, Oct. 6, 13, 1755.
[33]N. Y. Gazette and Weekly Mercury, Jan. 1, 8, 15, 22, 29, 1770.
[34]Pennsylvania Gazette, Sept. 30, 1772.
[35]N. Y. Mercury, May 6, 13, 20, Sept. 30, Oct. 7, 1765.

Week."[37] Examinations were conducted by Francis Daymon, of Philadelphia, in 1771, "in the presence of competent judges."[38] Thomas Carroll, of New York City, in 1765, invited "Gentlemen to visit his School, and be Judges of the Progress his Pupils will make, and the Benefit they must receive from him."[39]

[36]Pennsylvania Gazette, Oct. 25, 1770.
Theophilus Grew, and Horace Jones, Phila., 1753: "they do not intend many Scholars." (Ibid, Sept. 20, 27, 1753.)
John Beard, Phila., 1783: "He will take but twenty-five scholars, and he thinks he will be able to learn so small a number more in one quarter than they would be able to learn in a year at a school where there are sixty or seventy, as he will have so much time to attend to them and do the height of justice to each scholar; they must be well recommended before he will admit them to school." (Ibid, Nov. 12, 19, 1783.)
[37]Ibid, Sept. 18, 1766.
[38]Ibid, Oct. 3, 1771.
[39]N. Y. Mercury, May 6, 13, 20, Sept. 30, Oct. 7, 1765.

CHAPTER V

TUITION FEES

Available records contain but little information concerning the rates of tuition in the evening schools. An examination of 186 separate source-references to evening schools in New York City, between the years 1690 and 1783, revealed but one definite indication of fees; some 84 Philadelphia advertisements, of the years 1734-1783, yielded six; and the New England, and Southern newspapers contained two references to fees.

In most of the public announcements nothing more definite appears than such statements as "reasonable," "at reasonable Rates," and "upon very reasonable Terms." Equally unenlightening are the advertisements of masters who made a practice of "agreeing" with their students on the rates of tuition. The following notice, which appeared in the *New York Gazette*, August 31-September 7, 1730, is illustrative of this custom:

On the 15th of September next, at the Custom House in this City (where a convenient Room is fitted up) James Lyde designs to Teach in the Evenings (during the Winter) Arithmetick, in all its parts, Geometry, Trigonometry, Navigation, Surveying, Gauging, Algebra, and sundry other parts of Mathematical Learning, Whoever inclines to be instructed in any of the said Parts of Mathematical Knowledge, may agree with the said James Lyde at the House of William Bradford in the City of New York.

A Philadelphia master, in 1757, who offered the same courses, with the addition of "Merchants Accompts according to the true Italian Method of Dr. and Cr. by Double Entry," announced that "Young Gentlemen inclining to improve themselves in those Branches of Knowledge, may agree for the Winter Season, or otherwise, at a reasonable Rate, with said Morton."[1] There must have been uniformity, however, at certain periods, for some of the masters advertised that they would teach their various subjects "at the usual Rates."

The New York record, mentioned at the opening of the chapter, informs us that Robert Leeth, in 1752, taught "Writing at 8s. per Quarter, and vulgar and decimal Arithmetick at 10s."[2] Some light

---

[1]Pennsylvania Gazette, Oct. 20, 1757.
[2]N. Y. Gazette Revived in the Weekly Post Boy, Sept. 18, 25, Oct. 2, 9, 16, 23, 30, 1752.

may be thrown upon the tuition-fees of Connecticut, in 1774, by the following notice:

EVENING SCHOOL

For ALGEBRA, and those useful (though neglected) Rules in Arithmetic, VULGAR and DECIMAL FRACTIONS, the PROGRESSIONAL Series, the EX-TRACTION of the ROOTS, &c. The Subscriber proposes to teach provided not less than Ten, at one Shilling Lawful Money, per week, each, will engage, and attend their humble Servant,

Norwich, Conn.   Thomas Eyre.[3]

John Vinal, of Boston, in 1756, offered "Writing, Vulgar and Decimal Arithmetick, &c. &c. . . at Eight Shillings per Quarter."[4] The "Price" announced by Joseph Ward, also of Boston, in 1772, for "Writing, Arithmetic, English Grammar, Logic, and Composition" was "15s. per Quarter."[5] Ward adds that "No Fire Money nor Entrance will be required." Most of the evening school notices do not mention fire, and entrance fees; they were required only by the day schools. Ebenezer Dayton, of Newport, Rhode Island, in 1768, taught "Writing and Arithmetick, at Six Shillings, Lawful Money, per Quarter."[6] The only Charleston, South Carolina, reference is to "A French Evening School for young Gentlemen at 40s. per Month."[7]

In Philadelphia, Theophilus Grew, in 1734, advertised that "He teaches Writing and Arithmetick at the usual Rate of 10s. per Quarter. Merchants Accompts, Navigation &c. for 30s. per Quarter."[8] The rate for "Writing in all the hands of use; arithmetick, vulgar and decimal; merchants accounts; psalmody" in William Dawson's evening school, in 1753, was "Seven Shillings and Sixpence a quarter."[9] William Thorne gave notice, in 1766, that "ON Monday next, being the 13th Instant, will be opened an EVENING SCHOOL, for the Instruction of Youth in Writing, Arithmetic (Vulgar and Decimal) Merchants Accompts, Mensuration, Surveying, Gauging, Navigation, &c.," to which he added the following: "N. B. To prevent Trouble, the Price is 12s. 6d. per Quarter, Pens, Ink and Firing included."[10] An addendum of similar phraseology is attached to Lazarus Pine's announcement, in 1770, that "ON

[3]Norwich Packet, and Conn., N. H., and R. I. Weekly Advertiser, Dec. 1, 8, 1774.

[4]Boston Gazette and Country Journal, Sept. 13, 27, 1756.

[5]Mass. Gazette and Boston Weekly News Letter, Oct. 1, 15, 1772.

[6]Newport Mercury, Oct. 24-31, Oct. 31-Nov. 7, 1768; Feb. 27-Mar. 6, 1769.

[7]John Fouquet (South Carolina Gazette, Nov. 12, 19, 1744).

[8]American Weekly Mercury, Oct. 3-10, 17-24, Oct. 31-Nov. 7, Dec. 5-12, 1734; Oct. 16-23, 1735.

[9]Pennsylvania Gazette, Apr. 5, 12, May 3, 31, June 14, 28, 1753.

[10]Ibid, Oct. 9, 16, 1766.

Monday the 9th of October . . . will be opened an EVENING SCHOOL, where will be taught Writing and Arithmetic." It reads: "N. B. To prevent Trouble, the Price will be Ten Shillings and Six-pence a Quarter, Quills and Firing included."[11]

In 1772 a uniform rate was established for instruction in certain subjects, in the evening schools of Philadelphia. Evidently this was disregarded by Lazarus Pine, who continued to charge "Ten Shillings and Six-pence a Quarter."[12] But he was soon convinced that his fee was too low, and his fellow craftsmen in the city induced him to accept the schedule on which they had agreed. This interesting agreement was published in the *Pennsylvania Gazette*, September 30, 1772:

THE Schoolmasters of this city and district beg leave to inform the Public, that they intend opening NIGHT-SCHOOLS, at their respective school-houses, on Monday Evening, the 5th of October next, for the instruction of youth in READING, WRITING and ARITHMETIC, with the most useful branches of the MATHEMATICS. And to prevent all altercations, the price for reading, writing, and arithmetic will be 12/6 per quarter, Mathematics at the usual prices. - - - Whereas at a meeting of the Schoolmasters, held in this city, for the purpose of regulating the price of Night-schools, it appeared that Mr. *Lazarus Pine* had prior to the meeting, agreed with some persons upon lower terms than those agreed on by the meeting; this is to give information to such persons, that said *Pine* has come into the agreement; It is therefore hoped that such persons will not take amiss his uniting with the measures of his brethren, expecially as the odds can be but *Two Shillings* at the most.

Philadelphia   By Order of the Meeting
September 30, 1772.   ANDREW PORTER

The incompleteness of the sources just cited suggests the desirability of making a brief examination of some of the day school records. Advertisements indicating the rates of tuition in the day schools are more numerous, and it may be interesting to turn to these for purposes of comparison.

An unknown master of a day school, in New York City, announced, in 1735, that he "teaches Reading, Writing, and Arithmetick, at very reasonable Terms, which is per Quarter for Readers 5s. for Writers 8s. for Cypherers 1s."[13] In 1737, Joshua Ring, also of New York City, offered "Reading, Writing and Arithmetic at 12s. per Quarter; Reading and Writing at 10s."[14] Robert Leeth, in his day school, in 1752, taught "Writing at 9s. per Quarter; Vulgar and Decimal Arithmetick at 12s."[15] Leeth's fees do not differ very much from those of John Young, who announced, in 1766, that he "con-

---

[11]Pennsylvania Gazette, Sept. 27, 1770.
[12]Ibid, Sept. 26, 1771.
[13]N. Y. Gazette, July 14-21, 21-28, July 28-Aug. 4, 4-11, 1735.
[14]N. Y. Weekly Journal, Apr. 4, 11, 1737.
[15]N. Y. Gazette Revived in the Weekly Post Boy, Sept. 18, 25, Oct. 2, 9, 16, 23, 30, 1752.

tinues to teach as usual, Reading at 9s., Writing at 11s., and Arithmetic at 13s. per Quarter."[16] Another New York City rate was published by Amos Bull, in 1776, who taught "English Grammar, Reading, Writing, and Arithmetic . . . at 25s. per Quarter for each Scholar."[17]

The unsatisfactory character of the references renders it equally impossible to make any definite statements concerning the fees for the languages, and the "higher Branches." M. Langloiserie, of Boston, in 1738, gave instruction in French "at the Rate of Twenty Shillings a Quarter."[18] A New York City master, in 1735, also "taught the French and Spanish Languages . . . for 20s . per Quarter,"[19] and another, in 1775, offered "French and other languages . . . at very reasonable rates," which were £2 "a piece (½ entrance) a quarter."[20] The rates for the more advanced subjects were higher than those for the "lower branches," and the languages. Robert Leeth, in 1752, taught "BOOK KEEPING after the true Italian Method for 4£. The Art of Navigation for 3£,"[21] and John Young, also of New York City, in 1766, announced "common Accounts for 40s. Merchants ditto, after the Italian Method for £4."[22] In Philadelphia, Simon Williams, in 1759, offered English, Merchants Accounts, Mathematics, Greek, Latin, Geography, Rhetoric, Poetry, History, Moral Philosophy, and Physics at the rate of "Twenty Shillings per Quarter . . . and Twenty Shillings Entrance."[23]

For obvious reasons, tuition rates could not be uniform for all colonies. The expression "at the usual Rates" would seem to indicate that the fees in any particular city did not differ very much in any one-year period. A unique Philadelphia record, quoted above, indicates that, in 1772, the schoolmasters of that city entered into an agreement concerning the fees for the various subjects taught in the evening schools.

[16]N. Y. Mercury, May 19, 26, 1766.
[17]N. Y. Gazette and Weekly Mercury, May 13, 20, 1776.
[18]Boston Gazette, June 12, 19, 1738.
[19]N. Y. Gazette, July 14-21, 21-28, July 28-Aug. 4, 4-11, 1735.
[20]Francis Vandale: "a day and evening school." (Rivington's N. Y. Gazetteer or Conn., N. J., H. R., and Quebec Weekly Advertiser, Oct. 26, Nov. 9, 16, 1775.)
[21]N. Y. Gazette Revived in the Weekly Post Boy, Sept. 18, 25, Oct. 2, 9, 16, 23, 30, 1752.
[22]N. Y. Mercury, May 19, 26, 1766.
[23]Pennsylvania Gazette, Aug. 16, 1759.

CHAPTER VI

THE "SCHOOL HOUSE"

The school-buildings, and class-rooms were, in most cases, the same as those used by the day schools of the period. In many instances this double use is indicated in school-advertisements. Edward Willett, of New York City, announced, in 1757, that "A Day and Night School will be open'd."[1] On November 23, 1761, Thomas Johnson, also of New York City "begs Leave to inform the Public that he has this Day open'd a Day and Evening School."[2] William Dawson, of Philadelphia, advertised "a Day and Night School," in 1760.[3] There were many masters, however, who taught only in the evening.

The records do not contain the materials for a complete description of the school-house, or its equipment. In most instances they refer to "a School," "an Evening School," or "a Night School." Classes were often conducted in a "room," rented for that purpose. William Milne, of Philadelphia, in 1751, kept a "NIGHT SCHOOL . . . in his room, up an outer stair, in Albridge's Alley, at the sign of St. Andrew, opposite the shop of Nathan Trotter, Blacksmith, in Second-street, between Market and Chestnut-street."[4] Another Philadelphia evening school, in 1772, was provided with "two large rooms on the same floor."[5] John Nathan Hutchins, of New York City, in 1763,[6] and Ebenezer Dayton, of Newport, Rhode Island, in 1769, also had two rooms.[7] That the rooms were equipped for school purposes is indicated by James Lyde, of New York City, who announced, in 1730, that his evening school would meet "at the Custom House in this City (where a convenient Room is fitted up)."[8] Robert Leeth, also of New York City, gave evening instruction, in 1751,

---

[1]N. Y. Gazette or Weekly Post Boy, Oct. 14, 1757.
[2]N. Y. Mercury, Nov. 23, 1761.
[3]Pennsylvania Gazette, Nov. 20, Dec. 4, 1760.
[4]Ibid, Oct. 17, 24, 1751.
[5]Ibid, Sept. 30, 1772.
[6]N. Y. Mercury, Apr. 25, May 2, 1763: "provided with two convenient Rooms."
[7]Newport Mercury, Feb. 27-Mar. 6, 1769: "has two convenient Rooms."
[8]N. Y. Gazette, Aug. 31-Sept. 7, 1730.

"in a large commodious Room at Mr. Brown's a Taylor in Stone-Street."[9]

A Philadelphia evening school of 1745 was housed "In the Sail Loft, late belonging to Mr. William Chancellor."[10] Somewhat more pretentious was the establishment of "MR. DOVE, English Professor at the Academy," in Philadelphia, who, in 1752, "finding his former house too little for the number of his boarders," acquired "Rock Hall, which is situated in a wholesome air, for the reception of young gentlemen at board, washing, and lodging."[11]

Frequently the evening school occupied a "School-House." William Dawson, and John Gladstone, in Philadelphia, in 1756, conducted "an Evening School . . . at the School-House where Mr. Stephen Vidall formerly taught."[12] The "New School House, over against the New-Market," in Philadelphia, was used by William Ranstead, in 1756.[13] Other Philadelphia evening school masters met their classes "At the SCHOOL HOUSE, in Second-Street. Near the Corner of Chestnut-street,"[14] "at the new School-House in Fifth-street, a few doors above Market-street,"[15] and "at the OLD SCHOOL HOUSE in Arch-street."[16] A Philadelphia advertisement of 1766 announced that "AT the new Academy, in second-street, near Walnut-street, on Monday, the 29th Instant, will be opened an Evening Seminary."[17] John Wilson informed "The PUBLIC" that he had "opened a NIGHT SCHOOL," in 1772, "At the Academy in Newark, New Castle-County."[18]

As in the case of most school-houses, throughout the colonial period, these were erected privately, as commercial ventures, and rented to schoolmasters. A Philadelphia "Night School," of 1760, used "Mr. William's School-house, in Videll's Alley, Second-street."[19]

[9] N. Y. Evening Post, May 27, June 3, 1751.

John Searson (N. Y. Gazette or Weekly Post Boy, Sept. 15, 19, 29, Oct. 6, 13, 1755); James Wragg (Ibid, Apr. 7, 21, May 5, 1755).

[10] Pennsylvania Gazette, Aug. 15, 22, 29, 1745.

[11] Ibid, Jan. 7, 14, 21, Feb. 4, 18, Mar. 3, 17, Apr. 2, May 7, June 4, 18, July, 2, 30, Aug. 30, 1752.

[12] Ibid, Sept. 30, Oct. 14, 1756.

[13] Ibid, Nov. 25, 1756.

[14] Ibid, Sept. 8, Dec. 8, 22, 1757. James Cosgrove.

[15] Ibid, Sept. 27, 1770. Lazarus Pine.

[16] Ibid, Sept. 27, 1770. Joseph Stiles.

William Oliphant, Phila., 1770: "an EVENING SCHOOL...at the OLD SCHOOL HOUSE in Third-street." (Ibid, Sept. 27, 1770.)

[17] Ibid, Sept. 18, 1766.

[18] Ibid, Dec. 9, 1772.

[19] Robert Kennedy, John Maxfield, and David Kennedy. (Ibid, Sept. 18, 25, Oct. 2, 1760.)

Some of the masters may have owned the buildings which they occupied. Robert Cather, of Philadelphia, in 1756, offered evening instruction "at his School-house in Front-street, on Society-hill."[20] The phrases "at his School-House," and "at the Subscriber's school-house" occur frequently in evening school announcements.

Occasionally the Town School, and the Town Hall were rented by evening school masters. "Notice" was given by John Vinal, of Boston, in 1756, "That an EVENING SCHOOL will be opened the Third Day of October at the South Writing School."[21] Twenty years later, John Vinal appeared in Newburyport, Massachusetts, where he conducted an "EVENING SCHOOL . . . at the North School House."[22] In the same year, Nicholas Pike, also of Newburyport, announced that he would "open his EVENING SCHOOL at the Town House."[23] John Sims, "Schoolmaster in the Town-School," of Newport, Rhode Island, in 1759, met his evening classes in the same building.[24]

[20]Pennsylvania Gazette, Mar. 25, 1756.
[21]Boston Gazette and Country Journal, Sept. 13, 27, 1756.
Boston Post Boy and Weekly Advertiser, Oct. 9, 1758.
[22]Essex Journal and New Hampshire Packet, Oct. 25, Nov. 1, 1776.
[23]Ibid, Oct. 25, Nov. 1, 1776.
[24]Newport Mercury, May 22, June 5, 1759.

CHAPTER VII
THE SCHOOLMASTERS

From a professional standpoint, there was nothing peculiar about the masters of the evening schools. They were respectable members of the teaching profession of the period, and, as such, possessed the qualifications that were accepted at that time. Many of them appear to have had adequate preparation for their calling.

Some were college graduates: John Walton, of New York City, called attention to the fact that he was "late of Yale Colledge,"[1] and Anthony Fiva, also of New York City, that he had "had an academical education."[2] Nicholas Pike, of Newburyport, Massachusetts, graduated from Harvard with the class of 1766,[3] and John Beard, of Philadelphia, was a graduate of the University of Pennsylvania.[4] John Heffernan, of Philadelphia, advertised himself as "formerly of the College, and lately of the University of Pennsylvania."[5]

Others were teachers of experience, and made announcement of this qualification in their public notices. Andrew Lamb, of Philadelphia, had "taught Navigation, and kept a Journal above 40 Years."[6] A New York City schoolmaster, who opened an evening school in 1775, had "taught French and other Languages with good success, in Boston, and Newport in Rhode Island." He added that he "would

---

[1]Graduated from Yale in 1720. American Weekly Mercury, Oct. 17-24, 24-31, Oct. 31-Nov. 7, 1723.

[2]Rivington's N. Y. Gazetteer, or Conn., N. J., H. R., and Quebec Weekly Advertiser, July 22, Aug. 12, Dec. 9, 16, 1773.

John Haumaid had had "a regular education." (N. Y. Gazette and Weekly Mercury, Sept. 21, 1772.)

[3]Essex Journal and N. H. Packet, Oct. 25, Nov. 1, 1776.

[4]Class of 1759. (Pennsylvania Gazette, Oct. 8, 15, 22, 1783.)

[5]Pennsylvania Gazette, Sept. 14, 1774.

[6]Ibid, Oct. 23, Nov. 6, 1755.

Charles Fortesque, Phila., 1743: "late Free-School Master of Chester." (Ibid, Nov. 24, Dec. 1, 6, 15, 20, 1743.)

Joseph Ward, Boston, 1772: "has spent many Years in teaching Youth." (Mass. Gazette and Boston Weekly News Letter, Oct. 1, 15, 1772.)

Nathanael Platt, Phila., 1742, had been "Usher to the late Alexander Buller." (Pennsylvania Gazette, Mar. 31, Apr. 8, 1742.)

be glad to meet in New York the same encouragement."[7] James Cosgrove, of Philadelphia, in 1755, "who lately taught for Mr. Dove . . . professes to teach the Latin tongue, by the newest and most effectual methods, as he has not only been assistant to many worthy professors thereof, but also practised and taught the same for some years, to the Approbation of his employers, and others skilled therein."[8] The advertisements contain many statements to the effect that the masters had been "employed some years in the Instruction of Youth," or had "for some Years kept a private School in this City." A New York City master, in 1772, thought "it unnecessary to say anything respecting his abilities as a teacher, the bare mention of his having under his tuition the principal students of King's College . . . together with his having a regular education fully bespeaks his abilities as a teacher."[9]

Four of the evening school masters became teachers in the Philadelphia Academy. In 1750, the trustees appointed Theophilus Grew to teach mathematics, and David James Dove as "English Master." Dove had "taught grammar sixteen years at Chichester in England."[10] Horace Jones, who had been associated with Grew in an evening school venture, was appointed, in 1752, as his assistant in the Academy. In 1753, Andrew Morton was engaged as tutor in the Latin School of the Academy, where he served for six years.

Most of those who taught in the evening were also masters of day schools. Records of such instances are very numerous. Occasionally, a town-school master may have been given permission to offer evening classes as a private venture. John Sims, "Schoolmaster in the Town School" of Newport, Rhode Island, in 1759, proposed to open an evening school in the town school house.[11]

---

[7]Francis Vandale (Rivington's N. Y. Gazetteer, or Conn., N. J., H. R., and Quebec Weekly Advertiser, Oct. 26, Nov. 9, 16, 1775.)

John Philipse, New York City, 1758: "had the Honour of Teaching the Royal Family." (N. Y. Gazette or Weekly Post Boy, Jan. 30, Feb. 6, 20, Mar. 6, 1758.)

Anthon· Fiva, New York City, 1773: "resided many years in Paris and Madrid, he is therefore able to resolve any question that might puzzle his scholars." (Rivington's N. Y. Gazetteer, or Conn., N. J., H. R., and Quebec Weekly Advertiser, July 22, Aug. 12, Dec. 9, 16, 1773.) Fiva, 1774: "for these two years past has taught grammatically in this city, the English, French, Spanish, and Italian Languages, constantly with equal success." (Ibid, May 19, 26, 1774.)

[8]Pennsylvania Gazette, Feb. 4, 18, 1755.

[9]N. Y. Gazette and Weekly Mercury, Sept. 21, 1772.

[10]Benjamin Franklin, in a letter to Samuel Johnson, Dec. 24, 1751 (Beardsley, E. E. Life and Correspondence of Samuel Johnson, D. D., 1874, p. 166).

[11]Newport Mercury, May 22, June 5, 1759.

In some of the announcements attention is directed to the moral qualifications of the masters; they were men "of sober character, and qualified for the business," or "of good character." Some were ministers, or ex-ministers. Many of the masters who offered the practical courses were able to give their students the benefit of vocational experience. James Lamb, of New York City, in 1768, announced that "as he has had 16 Years Experience at Sea, flatters himself he can render Navigation (in some Measure) familiar to the young Navigator the first Voyage."[12] A Philadelphia teacher of navigation, in 1755, also claimed "great and long Experience at Sea, both on board the Royal Navy, and Merchant Ships."[13] Another Philadelphian, who taught book-keeping, in 1783, "was regularly bred to mercantile business, and several years in the practical part of book-keeping, in capital houses of trade in Europe."[14]

The teaching staff in most of the evening schools consisted of one master. Schools with two teachers were not uncommon, however, in New York City, and Philadelphia. In a New York City evening school, in 1747, Thomas Metcalfe had charge of "Reading, Writing, Arithmetic, Mathematics, &c.," while his partner taught "at the same place, in a separate Apartment . . . Greek, Latin, Rhetoric, Prosody."[15] "In order to do sufficient Justice to all who please to employ him," Alexander Power, of Philadelphia, in 1766, "chose for a partner Mr. JOHN DOWNEY, a Gentleman of good Character, and perhaps the ablest Mathematician who teaches in this Province."[16] Power was assisted, in 1772, by his brother William.[17] One of the brothers, whose first name is not indicated in the record, was in partnership, in 1771, with Matthew Maguire.[18] The records, at hand,

[12]N. Y. Gazette or Weekly Post Boy, Dec. 12, 1768.
[13]Pennsylvania Gazette, Oct. 23, Nov. 6, 1755.
[14]Ibid, Nov. 12, 19, 1783. George Fitzgerald.
[15]N. Y. Evening Post, Aug. 3, 1747.
Also in New York City: Benjamin Leigh, and Garrat Noel, 1751 (N. Y. Gazette Revived in the Weekly Post Boy, Jan. 21, 28, 1751); Edward Willett, and George Adams, 1758 (N. Y. Gazette, or Weekly Post Boy, Aug. 14, 28, Sept. 4, 1758); James, and Samuel Giles, 1759 (Parker's N. Y. Gazette, or Weekly Post Boy, Apr. 30, May 14, 21, 28, 1759); Gollen, and Mountain, 1774 (Rivington's N. Y. Gazetteer, or Conn., N. J., H. R., and Quebec Weekly Advertiser, Oct. 6, 1774).
[16]Pennsylvania Gazette, Oct. 2, 9, 1766.
Andrew Porter, Phila., 1771, had "a well qualified assistant." (Ibid, Nov. 21, 1771.)
Also in Phila: N. Walton, and W. Hetherington, 1745 (Ibid, Aug. 15, 22, 29, 1745); Theophilus Grew, and Horace Jones, 1753 (Ibid, Sept. 20, 27, 1753); William Dawson, and John Gladstone, 1756 (Ibid, Apr. 15, Sept. 30, Oct. 14, 1756).
[17]Ibid, Sept. 30, 1772.
[18]Ibid, Sept. 12, 1771.

reveal but two evening schools, both in Philadelphia, which had more than two teachers: one, in 1757, conducted by "JAMES COSGROVE with Assistants,"[19] and the other, in 1760, by Robert Kennedy, John Maxfield, and David Kennedy.[20]

It was not unusual for schoolmasters to engage in remunerative employments during their "spare time." Many must have found it necessary to supplement incomes derived from tuition-fees.

The book-store, for school-texts, and other books, was a common adjunct of the school. This enterprise may have suggested, occasionally, the sale of other commodities. Not infrequently the records refer to evening school masters who sold quills, slates, compasses, stationery, ink-powder, "instruments for marking linen," rum, brandy, "sweeted chocolate," tobacco, snuff, "fever pills," and flax.[21] "Book-binding of all sorts . . . in the best Manner was done by two Philadelphia masters: John Schuppy, 1743-1745,[22] and William Dawson, in 1756.[23]

Three of the masters, mentioned in this study, were authors of text-books. "The Youth's entertaining Amusement, or a plain Guide to Psalmody," by William Dawson, appeared in Philadelphia, in 1754. Two masters of Newburyport, Massachusetts, who taught before the Revolution, published arithmetics early in the state period: "A New and complete system of arithmetic," by Nicholas Pike, in 1788, and John Vinal's "Preceptor's Assistant," in 1792. Christopher Colles, of Philadelphia, occasionally published the lectures that he gave on geography, pneumatics, and hydraulics.

"Merchants, attorneys, and others" frequently employed translators to handle their foreign correspondence. It was but natural that they should turn to schoolmasters for this service. Garrat Noel, of New York City, announced, in 1751, that he "translates Spanish in the most faithful and exact Manner."[24] Thomas Ross, in 1754, translated French, Low Dutch, and Latin.[25] Another New

---

[19]Pennsylvania Gazette, Sept. 8, Dec. 8, 22, 1757.
[20]Ibid, Sept. 18, 25, Oct. 2, 1760.
[21]Phila: William Milne, 1751; William Dawson, 1756; Jacob Ehrenzeller, 1756; Francis Daymon, 1771-1777; John Beard, 1783.
New York City: Garrat Noel, 1755; William Cockburn, 1764; George Robinson, 1770.
Boston: Pelham.
[22]Pennsylvania Gazette, Nov. 16, 24, Dec. 1, 15, 1743; Sept. 20, 27, 1744; Sept. 26, 1745.
[23]Ibid, Apr. 15, 1756.
[24]N. Y. Gazette Revived in the Weekly Post Boy, Sept. 2, 9, 16, 23, 1751.
[25]N. Y. Mercury, Oct. 7, 1754.

York City master, Anthony Fiva, who kept an evening school, in 1773, for instruction in French, Spanish, and Italian, translated "from anyone of the aforesaid languages into English, or either of the two others, with accuracy, dispatch, and secrecy for attorneys, merchants, &c."[26] Jacob Lawn, master of a "French Night School, in Philadelphia, "also translates the German, French and English languages."[27]

Two New York City masters, in 1764, sought employment, during their spare time, as surveyors. Samuel Giles advertised that "Draughts and Surveys of Lands are made, or copied by him in the neatest Manner, on Paper or Parchment, and Writing done at reasonable Prices,"[28] and William Cockburn that "Gentlemen may also have their Estates surveyed, and plans made in the neatest Manner."[29]

Occasionally, schoolmasters appeared as public accountants, or auditors. William Dawson styled himself "Writing Master and Accomptant,"[30] and Alexander Power "posts Books, and settles Executors Accompts &c. in his spare Time."[31] Robert Leeth, "Schoolmaster and Scrivener," of New York City, added the following to his announcement of May 27, 1751: "Writings also of all Sorts fairly transcrib'd, engross'd or exemplified, as well as Accompts drawn out, inspected, settled and truly adjusted."[32]

Schoolmasters were in constant demand as scriveners, and copyists. Those who were expert penmen were frequently called upon to draw up, and copy wills, conveyances, contracts, and other public documents. Garrat Noel advertised that he "draws Writings of any Sort in an authentic Manner, or will copy Letters or any Writings for Gentlemen or others, with the utmost Secresie and Dispatch,"[33] and Nicholas Barrington, that he "Also writes for Gentlemen between Schools, Bills, Indentures, Bonds, Leases, Deeds of Sale, Wills, &c. at very reasonable Rates."[34] "Deeds of Conveyances

[26]Rivington's N. Y. Gazetteer, or Conn., N. J., H. R., and Quebec Weekly Advertiser, July 22, Aug. 12, Dec. 9, 16, 1773.
[27]Pennsylvania Gazette, Sept. 24, 1783.
[28]N. Y. Gazette, or Weekly Post Boy, Apr. 12, 1764.
[29]Ibid, Jan. 12, Feb. 16, 1764.
[30]Pennsylvania Gazette, Sept. 19, Oct. 10, 1754.
[31]Ibid, Oct. 2, 9, 1766.
[32]N. Y. Evening Post, May 27, June 3, 1751.
John Fouquet, Charleston, S. C., 1744: "Writings fairly engrossed or copied." (S. C. Gazette, Nov. 12, 19, 1744.)
[33]N. Y. Gazette Revived in the Weekly Post Boy, Sept. 2, 9, 16, 23, 1751.
[34]Ibid, Nov. 13, 1752.

and other Instruments" were also "authentically drawn" by N. Walton, and W. Hetherington.[35]

An interesting criticism of this common practice was published by Hugh Hughes, of New York City, in the announcement of his intention to open a "Morning and Evening School," in 1767. "Whoever is pleased to favour this Scheme, may depend on being served with Fidelity; as there will be no Deeds, Bills, Bonds, &c. or any Kind of Writing done, but such as will have a direct Tendency to promote the general Good of the School, which has constantly been the principal View of the Instructor, and on which Account he has rejected every Thing that he thought would be incompatible with the Duty of a Teacher."[36] This may have been merely another form of advertising.

---

[35]Pennsylvania Gazette, Aug. 15, 22, 29, 1745.
P. Webster, Phila., 1766: "does all Sorts of Conveyancing." (Ibid, Dec. 18, 1766.)
[36]N. Y. Gazette, or Weekly Post Boy, Apr. 16, 23, 30, May 7, 14, 21, June 4, 1767.

CHAPTER VIII
THE STUDENTS

All classes in colonial society patronised the evening schools. According to the sources, at hand, they were attended by "young Gentlemen and others," and "young Ladies." In most of the public notices of the schools the term "young Gentlemen" referred to all young men. Properly speaking, however, this title was enjoyed only by youths of independent economic status, or the sons of well-to-do parents.

A certain number of such young men, never very large in the colonial period, were destined to enter college. They might prepare for the entrance examinations in the evening, as well as in the day schools. James Cosgrove, of Philadelphia, in 1757, offered courses of instruction "sufficient to fit them for . . . college."[1] Many of the well-informed men in the American colonies, however, did not attend the colleges, but received their formal training in private schools of sub-collegiate rank. An appreciable number of the evening schools offered instruction in all the subjects of the college curriculum of the day. A school of this type was kept by John Walton, in New York City, in 1723, who announced that "if any Young Gentlemen of the City will please to come in the Evening and make some Tryal of the Liberal Arts, they may have oppertunity of Learning the same Things which are commonly Taught in Colledges."[2]

Most evening school students were employed during the day. Many of the advertisements were definitely addressed to "those who cannot come in the Day time,"[3] "Persons as have not Leisure to attend at the customary School-Hours,"[4] or "young men that are

[1]Pennsylvania Gazette, Sept. 8, Dec. 8, 22, 1757.
[2]American Weekly Mercury, Oct. 17-24, 24-31, Oct. 31-Nov. 7, 1723.
[3]Theophilus Grew, Phila., 1734-1735. (American Weekly Mercury, Oct. 3-10, 17-24, Oct. 31-Nov. 7, Dec. 5-12, 1735; Oct. 16-23, 1735.)
   Peter de Prefontaine, Phila., 1746: "an evening school for the instruction of those who cannot come in the day-time." (Pennsylvania Gazette, Oct. 30, 1746.)
   Francis Daymon, Phila., 1773: "for those who cannot conveniently attend in the Day Time." (Ibid, Nov. 17, 1773.)
[4]James, and Samuel Giles, New York City, 1759. (Parker's N. Y. Gazette, or Weekly Post Boy, Apr. 30, May 14, 21, 28, 1759.)
   Dunlap Adems, New York City, 1763: "Those who cannot spare time in the day time." (N. Y. Mercury, Jan. 10, 17, 24, May 9, 16, 1763.)
   Charles Shimmin, Salem, Mass., 1772: "all Persons that cannot attend in the Day Time." (Essex Gazette, Dec. 8-15, 15-22, 1772.)

engaged in business in the day."[5] Apprentices, and others engaged in occupational activities, took advantage of this opportunity of improving themselves in the technique of their vocations. James Cosgrove, of Philadelphia, in 1755, announced that "apprentices and others may be taught at the usual hours of evening schools;"[6] and John Heffernan, in 1774, that he had "opened a Night School . . . where a few of the emulous sons of industry will be occasionally attended to, with vigilance and assiduity."[7] To these the evening school offered the means of qualifying for advancement, or of preparing to change from one kind of employment to another.

The evening school also made it possible for those "whose business may prevent them from attending in the day" to receive instruction in the liberal, or cultural subjects. A Philadelphia advertisement of September 18, 1766 announces an "Evening Seminary," in which "Those whose Employment or Business will not admit of daily receiving polite Education, may be taught the Languages."[8]

Records indicating that girls, and young women, attended the evening schools are by no means uncommon. In some of the schools they sat with the boys, in others they were instructed "in classes apart." Alexander, and William Power, of Philadelphia, gave notice, in 1772, that "Girls will be admitted at night school, and have a convenient place for themselves."[9] Jeremiah Theus, of Charleston, South Carolina, announced, in 1744, "to all young Gentlemen and Ladies inclinable to be taught the Art of DRAWING, That an Evening School for that Purpose will be open'd of the first of November next, at my House in Friend Street, where every Branch of that Art will be taught with greatest Exactness."[10] In a Salem, Massachusetts, notice, of October 25–November 1, 1774, "The young LADIES and GENTLEMEN of the Town are informed that Mr. Hopkins intends to

---

[5]John Beard, Phila., 1783. (Pennsylvania Gazette, Oct. 8, 15, 22, 1783.)
Pelham, Boston, 1748: "for the Benefit of those employ'd in Business all the Day." (Boston Evening Post, Sept. 12, 19, 26, 1748.)
John Nathan Hutchins, New York City, 1763: "Young Gentlemen, &c. that cannot attend at other times." (N. Y. Mercury, Apr. 25, May 2, 1763.)
[6]Pennsylvania Gazette, Feb. 4, 18, 1755.
[7]Ibid, Sept. 14, 1774.
[8]Ibid, Sept. 18, 1766.
[9]Ibid, Sept. 30, 1772.
Francis Daymon, Phila., 1771. (Ibid, Sept. 5, 1771.)
[10]South Carolina Gazette, Nov. 5, 1744.
Nathaniel, and Mary Gittens, Charleston, S. C., 1744: "an Evening School... for writing, arithmetic, and young Ladies to draw." (Ibid, Sept. 17, 1744.)

open an Evening School, Monday next, at 7 o'clock."[11] John Vinal, of Newburyport, Massachusetts, in 1776, announced that he "Intends to begin his EVENING SCHOOL for Youth of both Sexes the first Monday Evening in November next, at the North School House."[12]

As may be expected, there were many evening schools "for the reception of young Ladies only." Ebenezer Dayton, of Newport, Rhode Island, in 1768, kept a "morning and evening school . . . wholly for the Instruction of Young Ladies."[13] An announcement by William Dawson, of Philadelphia, in 1753, and repeated with but slight variation in 1755, and 1756, may be of interest:

On Monday, the ninth of April instant (by permission of Providence)
will be opened,
A School to teach writing in all the hands of use; arithmetic, vulgar and decimal; merchants accounts; psalmody, by a proper and regular method; for the amusement of such young ladies as are pleased to employ the summer evenings in those useful and necessary exercises, from the hour of 5 to 8; carefully taught, in Third-street, near the New Presbyterian Church, by   WILLIAM DAWSON.[14]

In his notice of 1755, Dawson states that "accounts" will be taught "by way of single entry."[15] Robert Cather, in the following year, proposed "to open an Evening School . . . for the instruction of young Ladies, in writing and arithmetic, and to improve them in the rules of spelling and reading with propriety,"[16] and Joseph Garner, also of Philadelphia, in 1766, announced an "Evening School, on the first of April next, for the Reception of young Ladies only, where will be taught English grammatically, Writing, Accounts."[17]

It must not be inferred, from the sources quoted in the preceding paragraph, that the "young Ladies" were limited in their choice of subjects. The Schoolmasters gave instruction in such courses as were demanded in the evening. Day school announcements indicate that all of the courses offered the boys were open to election by the girls, if they so desired.

---

[11]Essex Gazette, Oct. 25-Nov. 1, 1774.
Samuel Wadsworth, Salem, 1773 (Ibid, Jan. 26-Feb. 2, 1773).
Mr. Munson, Salem, 1773 (Ibid, Sept. 7-14, 1773).
Peter Donworth, Marblehead, 1774 (Ibid, Feb. 8-15, 15-22, 1774).
[12]Essex Journal and N. H. Packet, Oct. 25, Nov. 1, 1776.
Hugh Hughes, New York City, 1767: "It is imagined that this Plan may suit some of both Sexes, who attend other Places of Education at different Periods, for other Purposes." (N. Y. Gazette, or Weekly Post Boy, Apr. 16, 23, 30, May 7, 14, 21, June 4, 1767.)
[13]Newport Mercury, Oct. 24-31, Oct. 31-Nov. 7, 1768.
W. Harris, New London, Connecticut, 1776 (Conn. Gazette and Universal Intelligencer, May 14, 1776).
[14]Pennsylvania Gazette, Apr. 5, 12, May 3, 31, June 14, 28, 1753.
[15]Ibid, Apr. 10, 1755: "an evening school for young Ladies, &c."
[16]Ibid, Mar. 25, 1756.
[17]Ibid, Feb. 13, 1766.

CHAPTER IX

CONCLUSION

The evening schools were important institutions in the American colonies. Their varied curricula, including both liberal and vocational courses, were designed to meet the needs of "those who cannot come in the Day Time." During these "convenient hours," a large number of young men and women must have begun and ended their formal schooling. For others, the evening schools solved the problem of continuative education; they were, in that sense, the continuation schools of the colonial period.

In their extension of educational opportunity to those who were engaged in occupational activities during the day, they were, necessarily, democratic in character. They appeared in large numbers, and competition was keen to obtain and hold students. To all who could afford the small fees, they offered the opportunity of receiving instruction in any subject desired. There was no prescribed course of study to be taken by all; the students might pursue as many, or as few, subjects as they wished. The comprehensive curricula satisfied the requirements of those who had called the schools into existence, and kept pace with their expanding interests and demands. Additions were made to the courses of study as soon as they were indicated by popular needs.

Essentially city institutions, they were most numerous at the seaports. In these centers of population, the diversified interests of the trades, and of commerce both on land and sea, made their special demands on the schools. The schoolmasters responded by offering the "practical Branches," which early became the most popular courses in the evening schools. Thomas Carroll, of New York City, in 1766, conducted "a night school . . . where young men may be . . . qualified for business, either as mechanic, merchant, seaman, engineer, &c.," and James Cosgrove, of Philadelphia, in 1757, proposed "to fit them for the Sea, the College, or the Counting-house." Merchants, engineers, and shipowners soon began to demand that the young men entering their employ have this technical preparation. The evening schools played a significant part in raising the entrance requirements of many pursuits. Trade training, as such, was provided by the apprenticeship system, but that institution could not supply the higher, theoretical instruction that was now needed to prepare apprentices for the vocations.

The evening schools in the English colonies were private ventures. Town schools, and others supported by public moneys, were kept only during the day. That this extension of educational opportunity was a public responsibility, did not enter the colonial consciousness. It was left to individual initiative, and private enterprise to meet the situation created by the new demands that were made on the schools.

Established in the seventeenth century, and continuing, without interruption, to the present day, they have played a prominent part in the solution of the problem of providing education for all classes. The essential characteristics of evening school practice at the present time find their origins in the colonial period.

APPENDIX A

ILLUSTRATIVE EVENING SCHOOL ANNOUNCEMENTS

Philadelphia, 1743

To be TAUGHT by CHARLES FORTESQUE,
late Free-School-Master of Chester, at his House, in the
Alley commonly called
Mr. Taylors

THE Latin Tongue, English in a Grammatical Manner, Navigation, Surveying, Mensuration, Dialling, Geography, Use of the Globes, the Gentleman's Astronomy, Chronology, Arithmetic, Merchants Accompts, &c. The above to be taught at Night School as well as Day—He likewise intends for the future to instruct his Latin Scholars in Writing himself.

NOTE, He hath private Lodgings for single Persons.[1]

Boston, 1748

Mr. Pelham's Writing and Arithmetick School, near the Town House (during the Winter Season) will be open from Candle-Light 'till Nine in the Evening as usual, for the Benefit of those employ'd in Business all the Day; and at his Dwelling House near the Quaker's Meeting in Lindell's Row, All Persons may be supply'd with the best Virginia Tobacco cut, spun into the very best Pigtail, and all other Sorts; also Snuff, at the cheapest Rates.[2]

New York City, 1753

JOHN LEWIS, Schoolmaster, in Broad-Street, has begun NIGHT SCHOOL, and teaches Reading, Writing, Arithmetic, Navigation, Surveying, &c.[3]

---

[1]Pennsylvania Gazette, Nov. 24, Dec. 1, 6, 15, 20, 1743.
[2]Boston Evening Post, Sept. 12, 19, 26, 1748.
[3]N. Y. Gazette or Weekly Post Boy, Oct. 8, 15, Nov. 26, Dec. 3, 1753.

New York City, 1755

NOTICE is hereby GIVEN that
JOHN SEARSON

Who teaches School at the House of Mrs. Coon opposite to the Post Office, proposes (God Willing) to open an Evening School, on Thursday the 25th of this Instant September; where may be learn'd Writing, Arithmetic Vulgar and Decimal, Merchants Accounts, Mensuration, Geometry, Trigonometry, Surveying, Dialling, and Navigation in a short, plain, and methodical Manner, and at very reasonable Rates. Said Searson having a large and commodious Room, together with his own diligent Attendance, the Scholars will have it in their Power to make a good Progress in a short Time.[4]

Philadelphia, 1760

Philadelphia, September 18, 1760.

NOTICE is hereby given, that on Monday, the 6th of October, at Mr. William's School-house, in Videll's Alley, Second-street, will be opened a Night School, and there taught as follows, viz. READING, WRITING, and ARITHMETIC, VULGAR and DECIMAL; BOOK-KEEPING METHODIZED; the ELEMENTS of GEOMETRY and TRIGONOMETRY, with their Application to NAVIGATION, SURVEYING, DIALLING &c. ALGEBRA, with the Application of it to a Variety of PROBLEMS in ARITHMETIC, GEOMETRY, TRIGONOMETRY, CONIC SECTIONS, and STEREOMETRY. With the several methods of solving and constructing EQUATIONS of the higher kind. By ROBERT KENNEDY, JOHN MAXFIELD, and DAVID KENNEDY. N. B. The Latin and Greek will be also taught.[5]

New York City, 1765

Taught by Thomas Carroll, At his Mathematical School, in Broad-street, in the City of New York.

Writing, Vulgar and Decimal Arithmetic; the Extraction of the Roots; Simple and Compound Interest; how to purchase or sell Annuities, Leases for Lives, or in Reversion, Freehold Estates, &c. at Simple and Compound Interest; the Italian Method of Book-keeping; Euclid's Elements of Geometry; Algebra and Conic Sec-

---

[4]N. Y. Gazette or Weekly Post Boy, Sept. 15, 19, 29, Oct. 6, 13, 1755.
[5]Pennsylvania Gazette, Sept. 18, 25, Oct. 2, 1760.

tions; Mensuration of Superficies and Solids, Surveying in Theory, and all its different Modes in Practice, with two universal Methods to determine the Areas of right lined Figures, and some useful Observations on the whole; Also Gauging, Dialling, Plain and Spheric Trigonometry, Navigation; the Construction and Use of the Charts, and Instruments necessary for keeping a Sea-Journal (with a Method to keep the same, were the Navigator deprived of his Instruments and Books &c. by any Accident) the Projection of the Sphere, according to the Orthographic and Stereographic Principles; Fortification, Gunnery, and Astronomy; Sir Isaac Newton's Laws of Motion; the Mechanical Powers viz. The Balance, Lever, Wedge, Screw and Axes in Peritrochio explained, Being not only an Introduction necessary to the more abstruse Parts of Natural and Experimental Philosophy, but also to every Gentleman in Business.

He will lecture to his Scholars, every Saturday, on the different Branches then taught in his School, the Advantage of which may in a little Time, make them rather Masters (of what they are then learning) than Scholars. He invites Gentlemen to visit his School, and be Judges of the progress his Pupils will make, and the Benefit they must receive from him.

He will attend a Morning School in Summer from 6 to nine for young Ladies only, from Nine to Twelve and from Two P.M. to Five for all others who choose to attend; and a Night School from Six to Nine for young Gentlemen; or he will divide the Time in any other Way, if thought more agreeable. Young Ladies and Gentlemen may be instructed in the more easy and entertaining Parts of Geography with the true Method of drawing the Plan of any Country &c. without which they cannot properly be said to understand that useful Branch of Knowledge; during this Course, Care will be taken to explain the true Copernican or Solar System, the Laws of Attraction, Gravitation, Cohesion &c. in an easy and familiar manner, and if he is encouraged to purchase proper Apparatus, he will exhibit a regular Course of experimental Philosophy. He will not accept any but decent Scholars, nor crowd his School with more than he can teach at a Time. On this plan, if the Gentlemen of this City are convinced of the vast Utility it must be to the Youth here, and are of the Opinion that he may be a useful Member amongst them, and encourage him as such, he will do all in his Power to merit their Approbation, and give general Satisfaction; but if otherwise, he will accept of any Employment in the writing way, settling Merchants' Accounts, drawing Plans, & or of a decent Place in the Country till the Return of the Vessels from Ireland, to which he has warm Invitations. He must observe that he was not under the Necessity of coming here to teach, he had Views of living more happy, but some unforseen and unexpected Events have happened since his Arrival here, which is the Reason of his applying thus to the Publick.

N. B. Mrs. Carroll proposes teaching young Ladies plain work, Samples, French Quilting, Knotting for Bed Quilts, or Toilets, Dresden, flowering on Cat Gut, Shading (with Silk, or Worsted) on Cambrick, Lawn, and Holland.[6]

Philadelphia, 1771

An Evening School, by Maguire and Power, will be opened on Monday, the eighth of October next, at the School-room of said Maguire, in Second-street, near Lodge-alley; where will be taught with the greatest care and diligence, reading, writing, and arithmetic; the most useful branches of the mathematics, book-keeping, geography; the use of globes and maps; and how to make maps.[7]

Newark, Del., 1772

To the Public

JOHN WILSON

At the Academy in Newark, New-Castle County; has opened

A NIGHT-SCHOOL

Where can be taught English reading and writing, with propriety and elegance, geography, chronology, arithmetic, book-keeping, geometry, and the construction of logarithms, plain and spherical trigonometry, mensuration of superficies and solids, gauging, dialling, fortification, architecture, navigation, surveying, the projection of the sphere, the use of the globes, conic sections, gunnery, algebra, the theory of the pendulums, fluxions, &c. &c. by

JOHN WILSON.

A young man, well acquainted with the English tongue, might have a course of mathematical education, for attending some of the

---

[6]N. Y. Mercury, May 6, 13, 20, Sept. 30, Oct. 7, 1765.
Carroll's notices of (Ibid) May 19, 26, 1766 indicate that the school was actually established.
[7]Pennsylvania Gazette, Sept. 12, 1771.

lower classes, in the Day-school, which said Wilson continues, at the same place, as usual.[8]

New York City, 1781
EDUCATION
Evening School, by Mr. Davis
in Maiden Lane, No. 63.

Where is taught Reading, a grace of the schools,
Writing, Arithmetic by easy rules,
Book-keeping, Geometry, too very plain,
And Navigation to steer o'er the main:
Surveying and Mensuration as well,
With rare Algebra to make you excell.
All those—and more he has got in his plan,
To rouse the genius, and furnish the man.

The Pupils may depend on an easy, elegant, perspicuous expli-
cation of things, being the most conducive to rouse the genius, and
invigorate the thought, or to inspire the mind, with a true and lively
sense of what is taught, which cannot fail to enrich it with fruitful
ideas; and as they shoot will not only be cherished, but made to
flourish.[9]

---

[8]Pennsylvania Gazette, Dec. 9, 1772.
[9]Royal Gazette, Oct. 6, 1781.
Appended to Mr. Davis' notice of 1782, in the New York Gazette and Weekly
Mercury, Jan. 7, 14, Oct. 14, 21, 1782, is the following:
These lively fields pure pleasure do impart,
    The fruit of science, and each useful art,
Which forms the mind, and clears the cloudy sense,
    By truth's powerful pleasing eloquence.
Ye hopeful youths, be sensible of this,
    O! mark the fleeting time and profer'd bliss,
The only time when learning makes its way
    Thro' dark ignorance, brightning into day:
Bright'ning into day, you'll in knowledge shine
    Full orb'd with widsom to the human mind
Ye hopeful youths, come learn what he has told,
    Exalt your Minds, and be what ye behold;
While Genius soaring, great Heights explore,
    And grace your Talents with true Beauties o'er,
Till ornamented with the Flowers of Truth,
    Ye shine bright Patterns for unlearned Youth.

APPENDIX B

ONE HUNDRED TYPICAL EVENING SCHOOL CURRICULA
1723-1770

(Abbreviations: accts.- accounts, alg.- algebra, arith.- arithmetic, astr.- astronomy, bk-kp.- book-keeping (cf. mer. accts.- merchants accounts), chr.- chronology, dial.- dialling, Eng.- English, eth.- ethics, Fr.- French, gaug.- gauging, geog.- geography, geom.- geometry, Ger.- German, gram.- grammar, Gr.- Greek, gun.- gunnery, Heb.- Hebrew, hist.- history, Lat.- Latin, logs.- logarithms, logic, math.- "mathematics," mens.- mensuration, met.- metaphysics, nat. phil.- natural philosophy, nav.- navigation, Port.- Portuguese, read.- reading, rhet.- rhetoric, Sp.- Spanish, spell.- spelling, ster.-stereometry, surv.- surveying, trig.- trigonometry, writ.- writing.)

1723 (Walton, N. Y.): read., writ., arith., nav., geom., surv., Lat., Gr., Heb., eth., rhet., logic, nat. phil., met.

1724 (Grainger, Boston): writ., accts., math.

1727 (Grainger, Boston): writ., arith., bk-kp., nav.

1730 (Lyde, N. Y.): arith., geom., trig., nav., surv., gaug., alg.

1734 (Grew, Phila.): writ., arith., mer. accts., alg., geom., surv., gaug., trig., nav., astr.

1735 (Grew, Phila.): writ., arith., mer. accts., alg., geom., surv., gaug., trig., nav., astr., "also the Use of Globes, Maps, Planispheres, Scales, Sliding Rules, and all sorts of Mathematical Instruments."

1741 (Pelham, Boston): writ., arith.

1742 (Platt, Phila.): writ., arith.

1743 (Crellius, Phila.): Ger.
(Schuppy, Phila.): Fr., Ger.
(Fortesque, Phila.): Lat., Eng., nav., surv., mens., dial., geog., globes, astr., chr., arith., mer. accts.

1744 (Theus, Charleston, S. C.): drawing.
(Gittens, Charleston): writ., arith., drawing.
(Fouquet, Charleston): Fr.
(Grew, Phila.): geom., alg., nav., astr., surv., gaug.
(Schuppy, Phila.): Ger.

1745 (Walton, and Hetherington, Phila.): writ., arith., mer. accts.

1746 (de Prefontaine, Phila.): read., writ., arith.
1747 (Metcalfe, N. Y.): read., writ., arith., math.
1748 (Pelham, Boston): writ., arith.
1750 (Leigh, and Noel, N. Y.): read., writ., arith., bk-kp., nav.,
    geog., globes, Lat., Gr., Fr., Port., Sp., short hand.
    (Evans, N. Y.): read., writ., arith.
    (Wayne, N. Y.): read., writ., arith., nav., Lat.
    (Noel, N. Y.): read., writ., gram., arith., Sp.
1751 (Leeth, N. Y.): read., writ., arith., Lat.
    (Milne, Phila.): writ., arith., nav., mens., spell.
1752 (Barrington, N. Y.): read., writ., arith., nav., mer. accts.
    (Leeth, N. Y.): writ., arith.
1753 (Dawson, Phila.): arith., mer. accts., nav., mens.
    (Mayor, N. Y.): Fr., Lat., Gr.
    (Grew, and Jones, Phila.): writ., arith., accts., math.
    (Davenport, Phila.): writ., arith.
    (Lewis, N. Y.): read., writ., arith., nav., surv.
1754 (Stiles, Phila.): writ., arith., mer. accts., nav.
    (Dawson, Phila.): writ., arith., mer. accts., nav., gaug., mens.,
    "with the use of the Gunter's sliding-rule."
    (Ross, N. Y.): Fr. Low-Dutch, Lat., Eng., writ., read., arith.
    (Lewis, N. Y.): read., writ., arith., nav., surv.
    (Mayor, N. Y.): Fr., Lat., Gr.
1755 (Searson, N. Y.): writ., arith., mer. accts., mens., geom., trig.,
    surv., dial., nav.
    (Wragg, N. Y.): writ., arith., mer. accts., nav., surv., mens.,
    gaug., dial., astr.
    (Lamb, Phila.): writ., arith., mer. accts., nav., trig., astr.,
    surv., gaug.
    (Dawson, Phila.): writ., arith., accts.
    (Cosgrove, Phila.): read., writ., arith., mer. accts., Lat.
1756 (Vinal, Boston): writ., arith., "&c. &c."
    (Stiles, Phila.): writ., arith., "&c. &c."
    (Cather, Phila.): writ., arith., spell., read.
    (Ranstead, Phila.): read, writ., arith., nav., surv., mens.,
    ster., gaug.
    (Ehrenzeller, Phila.): Ger.
    (Dawson, and Gladstone, Phila.): nav., writ., arith.
    (Wragg, N. Y.): writ., arith., mer. accts., nav., mens., surv.,
    gaug., dial., astr., "&c."

1757 (Philipse, N. Y.): Fr.

(Willett, N. Y.): read., arith., writ., mer. accts.

(Morton, Phila.): writ., arith., mer. accts., alg.

(Cosgrove, Phila.): spell., writ., arith., mer. accts., surv., nav., math., globes.

1758 (Vinal, Boston): writ., arith., alg.

(Willett, and Adams, N. Y.): read., writ., arith., nav., gun., surv., mer. accts.

1759 (Jas., and Sam. Giles, N. Y.): writ., arith., mens., bk-kp., trig., nav., surv., gaug., alg., geom., conic sections, "&c."

(Sims, Newport, R. I.): read., writ., arith., geom., trig., nav.

(Vinal, Boston): arith., writ., alg., bk-kp.

1760 (Oliphant, Phila.): read., writ., arith., nav., mens.

(Kennedy, Maxfield, and Kennedy, Phila.): read., writ., arith., bk-kp., geom., trig., nav., surv., dial., alg., conic sections, ster.

(Dawson, Phila.): read., writ., arith., accts., geom., trig., nav., "with the solution of every Problem by the plain or sliding Gunter."

1761 (Johnson, N. Y.): read., writ., arith., mer. accts.

(Bruce, N. Y.): read., writ., arith.

(Young, N. Y.): read., writ., mer. accts.

(Oliphant, Phila.): read., writ., arith., nav., mens., "&c. &c."

1762 (Jas. Giles, N. Y.): writ., arith., "&c. &c."

(Johnson, N. Y.): read., writ., arith., mer. accts.

1763 (Towel, Newport): read., writ., arith., nav., gaug.

(Sam. Giles, N. Y.): writ., arith., mer. accts., trig., nav., surv., alg., geom., "&c. &c."

(Hutchins, N. Y.): writ., arith., geom., trig., surv., gaug., dial., mens., astr., nav., globes, "the use of all Sorts of Charts, Plain or Globular."

(Adems, N. Y.): writ.

1763 (Howland, Newport): read., writ., arith., nav.

1764 (Cockburn, N. Y.): arith., geom., mens., gaug., trig., nav., astr., geog., globes, dial., gun., fortification.

(Sam. Giles, N. Y.): read., writ., arith., mer. accts., alg., trig., nav., surv.

1765 (Carroll, N. Y.): writ., arith., bk-kp., geom., alg., conic sections, mens., surv., gaug., dial., trig., nav., gun., astr., fortification.

1766 (Garner, Phila.): Eng., writ., accts.
(McCain, Phila.): surv., nav.
(Oliphant, Phila.): writ., arith. math.
(Academy, Phila.): "the languages," math., mer. accts., writ., arith.
(Thorne, Phila.): writ., arith., mer. accts., mens., surv., gaug., nav.
(Alex. Power, Phila.): Eng., writ., arith., bk-kp., geom., mens., trig., surv., nav., geog., astr., alg., conic sections, fluctions.
(Ehrenzeller, Phila.): Ger.
(Webster, Phila.): geog., logic, Eng.
(Carroll, N. Y.): writ., arith., bk-kp., geom., alg., conic sections.
1767 (Griffith, Boston): writ., arith.
(Hughes, N. Y.): writ., arith.
1768 (Dayton, Newport): read., writ., arith.
(Lamb, N. Y.): read., writ., arith., nav.
(Griffith, Boston): writ., arith.
1769 (Dayton, Newport): read., writ., arith.
1770 (Pine, Phila.): writ., arith.
(Maguire, Phila.): read., writ., arith., accts.
(Stiles, Phila.) writ., arith., "&c."
(Oliphant, Phila.): writ., arith., math., mer. accts.
(Ellison, Phila.): writ., arith., nav., math.
(Fentham, Phila.): Fr.
(Thorne, Phila.): writ., arith., mer. accts., mens., gaug., surv., nav.
(Daymon, Phila.): Fr.
(Ehrenzeller, Phila.): Ger.
(Robinson, N. Y.): bk-kp.
(Girault, N. Y.): Fr.

AMERICAN EDUCATION:
ITS MEN, IDEAS, AND INSTITUTIONS
An Arno Press/New York Times Collection

Series I

Adams, Francis. **The Free School System of the United States.** 1875.

Alcott, William A. **Confessions of a School Master.** 1839.

American Unitarian Association. **From Servitude to Service.** 1905.

Bagley, William C. **Determinism in Education.** 1925.

Barnard, Henry, editor. **Memoirs of Teachers, Educators, and Promoters and Benefactors of Education, Literature, and Science.** 1861.

Bell, Sadie. **The Church, the State, and Education in Virginia.** 1930.

Belting, Paul Everett. **The Development of the Free Public High School in Illinois to 1860.** 1919.

Berkson, Isaac B. **Theories of Americanization: A Critical Study.** 1920.

Blauch, Lloyd E. **Federal Cooperation in Agricultural Extension Work, Vocational Education, and Vocational Rehabilitation.** 1935.

Bloomfield, Meyer. **Vocational Guidance of Youth.** 1911.

Brewer, Clifton Hartwell. **A History of Religious Education in the Episcopal Church to 1835.** 1924.

Brown, Elmer Ellsworth. **The Making of Our Middle Schools.** 1902.

Brumbaugh, M. G. **Life and Works of Christopher Dock.** 1908.

Burns, Reverend J. A. **The Catholic School System in the United States.** 1908.

Burns, Reverend J. A. **The Growth and Development of the Catholic School System in the United States.** 1912.

Burton, Warren. **The District School as It Was.** 1850.

Butler, Nicholas Murray, editor. **Education in the United States.** 1900.

Butler, Vera M. **Education as Revealed By New England Newspapers prior to 1850.** 1935.

Campbell, Thomas Monroe. **The Movable School Goes to the Negro Farmer.** 1936.

Carter, James G. **Essays upon Popular Education.** 1826.

Carter, James G. **Letters to the Hon. William Prescott, LL.D., on the Free Schools of New England.** 1824.

Channing, William Ellery. **Self-Culture.** 1842.

Coe, George A. **A Social Theory of Religious Education.** 1917.

Committee on Secondary School Studies. **Report of the Committee on Secondary School Studies, Appointed at the Meeting of the National Education Association.** 1893.

Counts, George S. **Dare the School Build a New Social Order?** 1932.

Counts, George S. **The Selective Character of American Secondary Education.** 1922.

Counts, George S. **The Social Composition of Boards of Education.** 1927.

Culver, Raymond B. **Horace Mann and Religion in the Massachusetts Public Schools.** 1929.

Curoe, Philip R. V. **Educational Attitudes and Policies of Organized Labor in the United States.** 1926.

Dabney, Charles William. **Universal Education in the South.** 1936.

Dearborn, Ned Harland. **The Oswego Movement in American Education.** 1925.

De Lima, Agnes. **Our Enemy the Child.** 1926.

Dewey, John. **The Educational Situation.** 1902.

Dexter, Franklin B., editor. **Documentary History of Yale University.** 1916.

Eliot, Charles William. **Educational Reform: Essays and Addresses.** 1898.

Ensign, Forest Chester. **Compulsory School Attendance and Child Labor.** 1921.

Fitzpatrick, Edward Augustus. **The Educational Views and Influence of De Witt Clinton.** 1911.

Fleming, Sanford. **Children & Puritanism.** 1933.

Flexner, Abraham. **The American College: A Criticism.** 1908.

Foerster, Norman. **The Future of the Liberal College.** 1938.

Gilman, Daniel Coit. **University Problems in the United States.** 1898.

Hall, Samuel R. **Lectures on School-Keeping.** 1829.

Hall, Stanley G. **Adolescence: Its Psychology and Its Relations to Physiology, Anthropology, Sociology, Sex, Crime, Religion, and Education.** 1905. 2 vols.

Hansen, Allen Oscar. **Early Educational Leadership in the Ohio Valley.** 1923.

Harris, William T. **Psychologic Foundations of Education.** 1899.

Harris, William T. **Report of the Committee of Fifteen on the Elementary School.** 1895.

Harveson, Mae Elizabeth. **Catharine Esther Beecher: Pioneer Educator.** 1932.

Jackson, George Leroy. **The Development of School Support in Colonial Massachusetts.** 1909.

Kandel, I. L., editor. **Twenty-five Years of American Education.** 1924.

Kemp, William Webb. **The Support of Schools in Colonial New York by the Society for the Propagation of the Gospel in Foreign Parts.** 1913.

Kilpatrick, William Heard. **The Dutch Schools of New Netherland and Colonial New York.** 1912.

Kilpatrick, William Heard. **The Educational Frontier.** 1933.

Knight, Edgar Wallace. **The Influence of Reconstruction on Education in the South.** 1913.

Le Duc, Thomas. **Piety and Intellect at Amherst College, 1865-1912.** 1946.

Maclean, John. **History of the College of New Jersey from Its Origin in 1746 to the Commencement of 1854.** 1877.

Maddox, William Arthur. **The Free School Idea in Virginia before the Civil War.** 1918.

Mann, Horace. **Lectures on Education.** 1855.

McCadden, Joseph J. **Education in Pennsylvania, 1801-1835, and Its Debt to Roberts Vaux.** 1855.

McCallum, James Dow. **Eleazar Wheelock.** 1939.

McCuskey, Dorothy. **Bronson Alcott, Teacher.** 1940.

Meiklejohn, Alexander. **The Liberal College.** 1920.

Miller, Edward Alanson. **The History of Educational Legislation in Ohio from 1803 to 1850.** 1918.

Miller, George Frederick. **The Academy System of the State of New York.** 1922.

Monroe, Will S. **History of the Pestalozzian Movement in the United States.** 1907.

Mosely Education Commission. **Reports of the Mosely Education Commission to the United States of America October-December, 1903.** 1904.

Mowry, William A. **Recollections of a New England Educator.** 1908.

Mulhern, James. **A History of Secondary Education in Pennsylvania.** 1933.

National Herbart Society. **National Herbart Society Yearbooks 1-5, 1895-1899.** 1895-1899.

Nearing, Scott. **The New Education: A Review of Progressive Educational Movements of the Day.** 1915.

Neef, Joseph. **Sketches of a Plan and Method of Education.** 1808.

Nock, Albert Jay. **The Theory of Education in the United States.** 1932.

Norton, A. O., editor. **The First State Normal School in America: The Journals of Cyrus Pierce and Mary Swift.** 1926.

Oviatt, Edwin. **The Beginnings of Yale, 1701-1726.** 1916.

Packard, Frederic Adolphus. **The Daily Public School in the United States.** 1866.

Page, David P. **Theory and Practice of Teaching.** 1848.

Parker, Francis W. **Talks on Pedagogics: An Outline of the Theory of Concentration.** 1894.

Peabody, Elizabeth Palmer. **Record of a School.** 1835.

Porter, Noah. **The American Colleges and the American Public.** 1870.

Reigart, John Franklin. **The Lancasterian System of Instruction in the Schools of New York City.** 1916.

Reilly, Daniel F. **The School Controversy (1891-1893).** 1943.

Rice, Dr. J. M. **The Public-School System of the United States.** 1893.

Rice, Dr. J. M. **Scientific Management in Education.** 1912.

Ross, Early D. **Democracy's College: The Land-Grant Movement in the Formative Stage.** 1942.

Rugg, Harold, et al. **Curriculum-Making: Past and Present.** 1926.

Rugg, Harold, et al. **The Foundations of Curriculum-Making.** 1926.

Rugg, Harold and Shumaker, Ann. **The Child-Centered School.** 1928.

Seybolt, Robert Francis. **Apprenticeship and Apprenticeship Education in Colonial New England and New York.** 1917.

Seybolt, Robert Francis. **The Private Schools of Colonial Boston.** 1935.

Seybolt, Robert Francis. **The Public Schools of Colonial Boston.** 1935.

Sheldon, Henry D. **Student Life and Customs.** 1901.

Sherrill, Lewis Joseph. **Presbyterian Parochial Schools, 1846-1870.** 1932 .

Siljestrom, P. A. **Educational Institutions of the United States.** 1853.

Small, Walter Herbert. **Early New England Schools.** 1914.

Soltes, Mordecai. **The Yiddish Press: An Americanizing Agency.** 1925.

Stewart, George, Jr. **A History of Religious Education in Connecticut to the Middle of the Nineteenth Century.** 1924.

Storr, Richard J. **The Beginnings of Graduate Education in America.** 1953.

Stout, John Elbert. **The Development of High-School Curricula in the North Central States from 1860 to 1918.** 1921.

Suzzallo, Henry. **The Rise of Local School Supervision in Massachusetts.** 1906.

Swett, John. **Public Education in California.** 1911.

Tappan, Henry P. **University Education.** 1851.

Taylor, Howard Cromwell. **The Educational Significance of the Early Federal Land Ordinances.** 1921.

Taylor, J. Orville. **The District School.** 1834.

Tewksbury, Donald G. **The Founding of American Colleges and Universities before the Civil War.** 1932.

Thorndike, Edward L. **Educational Psychology.** 1913-1914.

True, Alfred Charles. **A History of Agricultural Education in the United States, 1785-1925.** 1929.

True, Alfred Charles. **A History of Agricultural Extension Work in the United States, 1785-1923.** 1928.

Updegraff, Harlan. **The Origin of the Moving School in Massachusetts.** 1908.

Wayland, Francis. **Thoughts on the Present Collegiate System in the United States.** 1842.

Weber, Samuel Edwin. **The Charity School Movement in Colonial Pennsylvania.** 1905.

Wells, Guy Fred. **Parish Education in Colonial Virginia.** 1923.

Wickersham, J. P. **The History of Education in Pennsylvania.** 1885.

Woodward, Calvin M. **The Manual Training School.** 1887.

Woody, Thomas. **Early Quaker Education in Pennsylvania.** 1920.

Woody, Thomas. **Quaker Education in the Colony and State of New Jersey.** 1923.

Wroth, Lawrence C. **An American Bookshelf, 1755.** 1934.

Series II

Adams, Evelyn C. **American Indian Education.** 1946.

Bailey, Joseph Cannon. **Seaman A. Knapp: Schoolmaster of American Agriculture.** 1945.

Beecher, Catharine and Harriet Beecher Stowe. **The American Woman's Home.** 1869.

Benezet, Louis T. **General Education in the Progressive College.** 1943.

Boas, Louise Schutz. **Woman's Education Begins.** 1935.

Bobbitt, Franklin. **The Curriculum.** 1918.

Bode, Boyd H. **Progressive Education at the Crossroads.** 1938.

Bourne, William Oland. **History of the Public School Society of the City of New York.** 1870.

Bronson, Walter C. **The History of Brown University, 1764-1914.** 1914.

Burstall, Sara A. **The Education of Girls in the United States.** 1894.

Butts, R. Freeman. **The College Charts Its Course.** 1939.

Caldwell, Otis W. and Stuart A. Courtis. **Then & Now in Education, 1845-1923.** 1923.

Calverton, V. F. & Samuel D. Schmalhausen, editors. **The New Generation: The Intimate Problems of Modern Parents and Children.** 1930.

Charters, W. W. **Curriculum Construction.** 1923.

Childs, John L. **Education and Morals.** 1950.

Childs, John L. Education and the Philosophy of Experimentalism. 1931.

Clapp, Elsie Ripley. Community Schools in Action. 1939.

Counts, George S. The American Road to Culture: A Social Interpretation of Education in the United States. 1930.

Counts, George S. School and Society in Chicago. 1928.

Finegan, Thomas E. Free Schools. 1921.

Fletcher, Robert Samuel. A History of Oberlin College. 1943.

Grattan, C. Hartley. In Quest of Knowledge: A Historical Perspective on Adult Education. 1955.

Hartman, Gertrude & Ann Shumaker, editors. Creative Expression. 1932.

Kandel, I. L. The Cult of Uncertainty. 1943.

Kandel, I. L. Examinations and Their Substitutes in the United States. 1936.

Kilpatrick, William Heard. Education for a Changing Civilization. 1926.

Kilpatrick, William Heard. Foundations of Method. 1925.

Kilpatrick, William Heard. The Montessori System Examined. 1914.

Lang, Ossian H., editor. Educational Creeds of the Nineteenth Century. 1898.

Learned, William S. The Quality of the Educational Process in the United States and in Europe. 1927.

Meiklejohn, Alexander. The Experimental College. 1932.

Middlekauff, Robert. Ancients and Axioms: Secondary Education in Eighteenth-Century New England. 1963.

Norwood, William Frederick. Medical Education in the United States Before the Civil War. 1944.

Parsons, Elsie W. Clews. Educational Legislation and Administration of the Colonial Governments. 1899.

Perry, Charles M. Henry Philip Tappan: Philosopher and University President. 1933.

Pierce, Bessie Louise. Civic Attitudes in American School Textbooks. 1930.

Rice, Edwin Wilbur. The Sunday-School Movement (1780-1917) and the American Sunday-School Union (1817-1917). 1917.

Robinson, James Harvey. The Humanizing of Knowledge. 1924.

Ryan, W. Carson. Studies in Early Graduate Education. 1939.

Seybolt, Robert Francis. The Evening School in Colonial America. 1925.

Seybolt, Robert Francis. Source Studies in American Colonial Education. 1925.

Todd, Lewis Paul. Wartime Relations of the Federal Government and the Public Schools, 1917-1918. 1945.

Vandewalker, Nina C. The Kindergarten in American Education. 1908.

Ward, Florence Elizabeth. The Montessori Method and the American School. 1913.

West, Andrew Fleming. Short Papers on American Liberal Education. 1907.

Wright, Marion M. Thompson. The Education of Negroes in New Jersey. 1941.

Supplement

The Social Frontier (Frontiers of Democracy). Vols. 1-10, 1934-1943.